HAZEL EDWARDS

NOT JUST A PIECE OF CAKE
BEING AN AUTHOR

un

ABOUT *UNTAPPED*

Most Australian books ever written have fallen out of print and become unavailable for purchase or loan from libraries. This includes important local and national histories, biographies and memoirs, beloved children's titles, and even winners of glittering literary prizes such as the Miles Franklin Literary Award.

Supported by funding from state and territory libraries, philanthropists and the Australian Research Council, *Untapped* is identifying Australia's culturally important lost books, digitising them, and promoting them to new generations of readers. As well as providing access to lost books and a new source of revenue for their writers, the *Untapped* collaboration is supporting new research into the economic value of authors' reversion rights and book promotion by libraries, and the relationship between library lending and digital book sales. The results will feed into public policy discussions about how we can better support Australian authors, readers and culture.

See untapped.org.au for more information, including a full list of project partners and rediscovered books.

Readers are reminded that these books are products of their time. Some may contain language or reflect views that might now be found offensive or inappropriate.

CONTENTS

Chapter 1 · Anecdultery	1
Chapter 2 · Deadlines	5
Chapter 3 · Back To School Day	12
Chapter 4 · Literary Speed Dating	20
Chapter 5 · The Plateau Of Boredom	27
Chapter 6 · Story Stealing	31
Chapter 7 · General Store	35
Chapter 8 · Fan Mail	43
Chapter 9 · Highlights Of Hippo History	61
Chapter 10 · Choosing Apt Titles	75
Chapter 11 · Come And Meet My Camel	79
Chapter 12 · Is Writing Your Family Trade?	90
Chapter 13 · Family & Friends	95
Chapter 14 · Domestic Survival?	108
Chapter 15 · Mentoring, Mintees And Hazelnuts	116
Chapter 16 · Mystery Writing On Location	125
Chapter 17 · Do You Put Real People In Your Stories?	135
Chapter 18 · Banned, Controversial Or Just Difficult	141
Chapter 19 · Participant Observation	145
Chapter 20 · Trekking In Nepal	150
Chapter 21 · Antarctic Writer On Ice	156
Chapter 22 · Ideas Addict: Why Do You Write?	167
Chapter 23 · Why Collaborate?	169
Chapter 24 · Charitable Overload	173
Chapter 25 · 'Memorable' Author Visit	177
Chapter 26 · On Tour	189
Chapter 27 · Writing Heroes For Kids	193
Chapter 28 · Not Just A Piece Of Cake	198

ACKNOWLEDGEMENTS

Kim Edwards, Mich Layet
& photographer Mary Broome

West Sydney Library Cake

Hospital cake angels

Sharing the hippo cake, NT Parliament

CHAPTER 1
ANECDULTERY

A is for ... Author Anecdultery

Authors don't actually lie, they embellish. After they've told an anecdote a few times, they can't distinguish the raw material from the 'doctored' dramatised version. Is it dramatic licence or lying? Fiction or fraud? Creativity or crime?

Anecdultery it has been called. Children's authors are good at it. Embellishing and re-telling stories.

'When did you start reading?' is a frequent question on author visits to schools, libraries and conferences.

My usual answer is, 'Before I went to school. My grandma taught me.'

Now I think that is true—but I'm not absolutely sure about any early fact now. My grandmother read to me daily, as due to working parents she was my minder before and after school. I can remember being disappointed with the first day at school because they wouldn't let me take the new library books home. I'd been looking forward to a new supply of stories as I knew all my very Baptist Grandma's Biblical stories. The 'missionary' serials about Fijian and Chinese converts were 'gory' and I had to pretend to need to go to the toilet to miss the bloodthirsty bits. Grandma was convinced I had a weak bladder.

I can also remember a teacher, Miss Hugo from Grade 2, who yelled at me, accusing me of lying. Because I'd read all the beginners' books within the classroom library, I'd been permitted to 'borrow' one book from the Grade 2 shelves in the classroom next door. I chose carefully at 3.30 p.m. and returned it the next day to Miss Hugo.

'How dare you say you read this book last night. You're a liar! And you know what happens to little girls who tell lies.'

Certainly I knew all the Biblical odds about breaking the Ten Commandments. I never went near her classroom library shelves again, but it didn't stop my readaholism.

I remember her as an alarmingly large woman with a shelf of a bosom. Coincidentally, when I was 17, I recognised her on a city tram. I was now taller. She was tiny, but still with a shelf-like bosom which I imagined stacked with unread library books. Today I wonder, where she would carry e-books?

Authors have always claimed dramatic licence to 'play around' with events so the published stories are more interesting for the reader or viewer. I'm not just talking facts such as dates here, but more a matter of interpretation.

Unlike sportspeople who can measure how far or fast they run or swim, an author's challenges and viewpoints are only measurable by fans and their questions.

After running workshops on 'Writing a Non-Boring Family History', I'm aware of the dangers of egotistical exercises in chronological boredom which pass as autobiographies—especially (shipping) lists of 'begats' who married or didn't marry, the children's names and when they died. Dead, boring stuff.

Also I'm conscious of how relatives re-invent the past to make their present look acceptable. After a recent visit from an interstate relative, and long chats about common ancestors, I've realised that my interpretation of some relatives is entirely different. Some family history is just high-level gossip, repeated and rarely challenged.

Yesterday I realised that I am one of the few alive who remembers my parents and older relatives—but is my interpretation of them accurate, or have I manipulated memories?

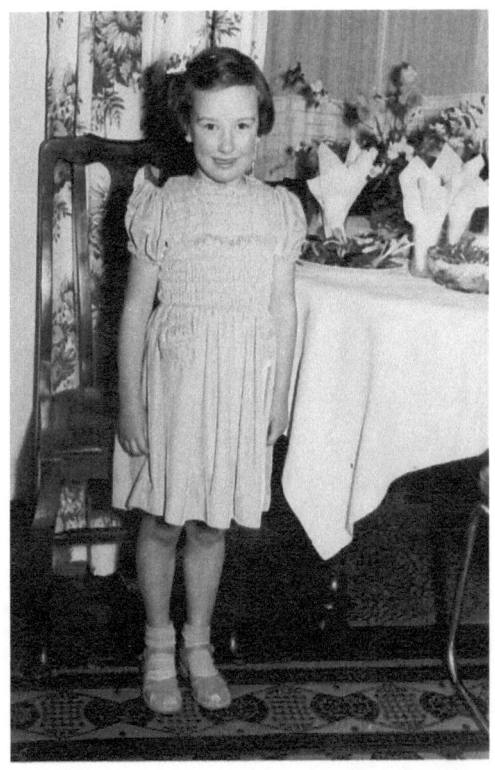

Reading Scene

My stock answer is, 'My grandma taught me to read before I went to school.'

I've said it so often now that I can't get my mind around a picture of it. Can I see her with the book in her hand? Can I see myself mouthing the words? No. Did I invent that just so I seem intelligent?

The only pictorial memory I have is frequently racing off to the outside—and slightly smelly—toilet near the well with the fig tree, as a means of getting away from some of mild-mannered Grandma's gory missionary stories.

That I do remember. But maybe I am committing Anecdultery?

CHAPTER 2
DEADLINES

Authors keep deadlines, mostly.

- Goal
- Time limit
- Cut-off date

Real life is more than Thesaurus word choice.

Lying in Emergency, linked to beeping devices, cut-off date seemed the most relevant type of deadline. I can spell 'cardiologist' but acquiring one was a worry. What if I were never able to write again? What mattered?

Luckily my deadline has been extended.

In early February I had flown home to Melbourne on the 'Red Eye' plane from the Darwin book launch of *Trail Magic: Going Walkabout for 2184 Miles on the Appalachian Trail*. I thought it was just the tropical heat getting to me.

To find that my heart wasn't working efficiently (as previously I considered it ran on willpower, not valves or pills) was fact, not fiction.

Gifts

What was real? My daughter sitting at my Emergency bedside for 7 hours—she was real. My 3-year-old grandson bringing a Band-Aid to fix grandma—he was real. So was the hospital gift of illustrator friend Ann James's original "Get Well" artwork (check out the strategic Band-Aid).

In a hospital, you look at ceilings a lot. Could book illustrations and cartoons be added to corridor ceilings as a gallery?

What if you were illiterate and couldn't read medical instructions on pill bottles? A mix up of patients, pills or problems? Potential murder plot?

Could you write in shadows across the walls ... ghost writer graffiti?

So many tests and x-rays. Could a sense of humour show up?

Not a dead end. Still a line of imagination working.

April 1st seems an apt date to begin a short, non-boring memoir about survival strategies as an author. But no deadline.

Drawn by Mike Spoor.

Dangers of the Memoir

Writing for children is not a piece of cake. Despite creating the vintage picture book *There's a Hippopotamus on Our Roof Eating Cake* which has only 404 words, and one less when 'smack' was censored out years later, brief writing is the hardest. Sub-text which suggests more than the surface words matters. So does choreographing the ideas.

That's why a brief memoir is more challenging than a birth-to-now-autobiography. A children's author is expected to be amenably 'nice', not candidly honest. But 'memoir' is an elastic term to cover any bits of your life about which you choose to write.

'How can you write kids' books when you are so old?' asked a six-year-old mathematician. 'We Googled. You are not six years old. You were born last century in 1945.'

'Vintage' is the 'in' word for old, veteran or antique. 'Child-like' means enthusiasm at any age, looking at things with fresh eyes. Not 'child-*ish*' which means self-absorbed and petulant. Big difference. Long term children's authors tend to suffer from optimistic curiosity i.e. child-like perception. Others call it naivety.

Dreaming in Fractals

For this memoir, I prefer a conversational format, including my meanderings to work out the answer for myself. I used to dream and think in fractals. Fractals are patterns in nature, like repeated structural shapes of ideas.

I'm not talking of just going around in circles—although I've done my share of that.

The hidden patterns in the PROCESS of the process of creativity will be my quest.

Why succumb now?

Sorting Memories in the Hippocampus.

I'm hopeless at filing and formatting. I think in abstract. Not visual. Need to write while I can remember quirky details or find them from less-than-perfectly-backed–up files, five computers ago. My worst fear is to lose my imagination, or the ability to play with ideas. Six years earlier, suddenly immobile with Streptococcus agalactiae Group B, this mysterious bug affected my ability to think in abstract or multi-plot fiction.

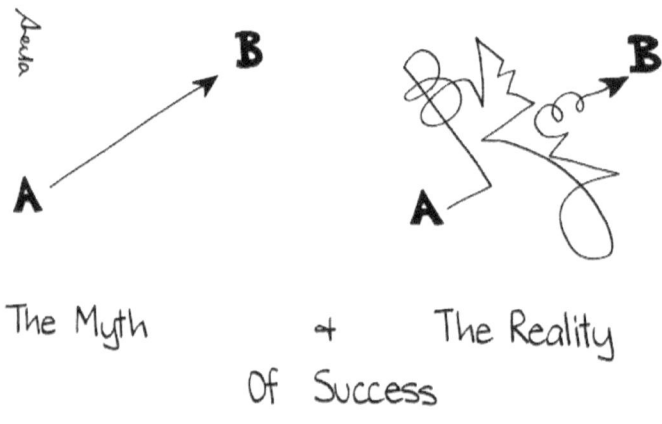

Sheila Hollingworth cartoon.

'Others just get the flu. Trust you to get an exotic, dramatic, unpronounceable medical condition!' said a friend.

Now I rarely dream in fractals but I'm mentally ok, despite being aware of early dementia crippling certain writers. I need to use my hippocampus, where memories are stored, NOW. This memoir attempts to re-capture the creative process as a participant observer.

As I de-clutter my study and throw out 'stuff', I get sidetracked by drafts I wrote years ago. A 'successful' project might look like an instant impulsive idea, but it's often founded on earlier discards.

Becoming an author is a process of detours, mistakes and

ad hoc decisions. Mainly wrong. The only benefit is you have experienced universal feelings, and can project these inadequacies onto your characters, which makes you a better author. Personal flaws are research, ironically. The best stories come from things going wrong—the gap between aspiration and workday reality.

It's helpful if a writer gets lost, is clumsy and makes mistakes: all of that is part of creative problem-solving.

Are memoirs fiction dressed up as fact? Maybe mine is faction because it is genuinely difficult for novelists to remember the exact details of a life, which may have been dramatised already as fiction. Or the sanitised versions offered during interviews where an author is asked, 'Why did you become a writer?'

'Because I wanted to experience a varied life, and see things from others' viewpoints.'

Histories are meant to be only verifiable facts. In memoirs, bias and ego creep in. That's the quandary. I prefer 'Questory' as a kind of historic quest for a story.

Most writers are unemployable. After a few years, we like to do things our own way—even freakishly control the worlds of our characters. We dabble in crime, on screen or on the page if not in real life, by breaking rules. In what other occupation could you change jobs, gender, age or location so often, at least within the book or script?

I've just reached that status of not wanting to have my life controlled by others. I'm too independent as long-term self-employed and yet emotionally vulnerable to criticism. There, I've admitted my first flaw—or is it my second?

What if I try to answer honestly about the influences which made me a writer? We like to know 'what went wrong' in a person's life and how they coped. It makes us all feel better about our own inadequacies. But how candid should honesty be? Especially if others are involved?

Which brings me to criticism.

Criticism

Those who write for children are assumed to have an IQ commensurate with the single-digit age of their readers. But, in fact, deceptively simple writing takes more skill. To make it sound simple, you really have to know your subject.

To be effective as a writer, you may have to reveal doubts, mistakes and genuine feelings, or the work will be superficial. Good writing analyses the depth of motivation and portrays flaws, with compassion. Revenge is not a good motivation: frustration might be. So, the 'selfie' bio needs to be a kind of 'honesty insurance policy' so the raw facts will be available. Or my version of them anyway. But it is a kind of emotional nakedness—nude writing which is nothing to do with keyboarding minus clothes.

Many choose to call their work fiction, even if it is heavily mined autobiography. They re-distribute their own flaws and anecdotes across a range of characters. This is less likely to cause legal challenges, even if readers play the 'hunt through the book to find my name' game. Or ask, 'Is there an index?' and 'Am I in it?'

Non-fiction should be verifiable. Historians may disagree with the interpretation but the dates and places need to be accurate. Difficult if you're the kind of autobiographer who only remembers by association, like, that was the year the bushfire swept through and burnt the records in the general store (made that up) or I got lost for six embarrassing hours while orienteering and had to have Search and Rescue find me (true). Or the year I trekked in Nepal, altitude sickness got me and I needed sherpa help to climb out of the mountains in the footsteps of a friend from the Spirited Women's Trek who led the way (that was true too).

I'm experimenting with a new style of writing for my 'soul' project—just anecdotal association. Things remembered which provoked other stories, which explain why I wrote, and write still. I could not live without writing to make sense of experience or understand the motivations of others. I went on an Antarctic expedition to find out whether expeditioners were running to adventure or running away from home. Answer? Read on.

Therapeutic writing allows a freedom to be candid and for ideas to flow, but commercial authors do have a duty to structure the story in a way that will entertain and inform the reader. That's their obligation for taking the reader's time and maybe their credit card.

Risk-taking

Free-lancing (originally medieval mercenary soldiers with a lance for hire, so they weren't free) is a high-risk artistic occupation, with a one-in-ten return on investment of energy and intellectual property (and less when international pirates pinch e-books). As others of my chronological age 'retire' and talk of wanting to write a book, I have had the privilege all my life of doing what others save for a hobby. As a children's author, it is acceptable to be 'eccentric' in clothes, habits and ideas, like the afternoon the incredulous Parisian puppeteer visited and exclaimed to me, in a delightful French accent, 'You are a writer and you live in suburbia!' 'The Map of Serendipity' is a title I've been saving for the juxtaposing of ideas. The structure of mapping but the happiness of fortuitous finding. In a selfie bio. Maybe 'selfie' will date and 'Questory' is more accurate?

CHAPTER 3
BACK TO SCHOOL DAY

Back to School Day, Tuesday May 17th 2005
Former Traralgon High student 1959–61 (Years 9, 10, 11)

No mobile phones, Internet or texting.

Just long school-bus rides with all-age country kids dropped off at different schools. The school bus was matchmaking on wheels. There were farm kids, town kids and the ones in between like me, whose parents ran the country general store so I knew all the gossip. A necessary apprenticeship for an author, as gossip about quirky stuff, not malicious tale-telling, is ground-level research.

Ashburton Primary School

'Trying to catch up' and 'being the outsider' were my major memories of secondary schooling. Because my father was ill, we moved a lot, so I went to four secondary schools and lived in two general stores. Books and passionate teachers were a way into other worlds.

I don't remember the buildings much because most were standard grey, and I was always getting lost in long corridors, but I do remember the love of learning which was caught from enthusiastic teachers.

A History & English teacher called Mr Mitchell and a Mr Terrill, who loved his maths, were inspirational. Plotting novels requires structure and the logic of mathematical thinking.

I also had an unusual father who encouraged reading and philosophical discussion in between trying to make a living in a seven-days-a-week country store. He valued school education for the access to ideas, but he encouraged other ways of learning too. I decided that being an author was a way of continuing to learn about new things and go to new places. It's been a great excuse for tramping the Milford Track in New Zealand, visiting a funeral parlour, hot-air ballooning and asking questions. 'Research' is the respectable label for being a professional 'stickybeak', which is an Australian colloquialism. The Americans call it 'being a nosy parker', as I discovered when speaking to New York students about my duck picture book *Stickybeak*. And they weren't keen on sampling my gift of the salty taste of Vegemite, which they expected to be sweet. Many mixed up Austria and Australia and were surprised I could write and speak in English. I was surprised at the local censorship of subjects in children's books. Small town thinking exists in all countries, but books are a way of entering wider worlds.

Although our family had no spare money, my father always bought me the full school uniform and all the books. I had grey, green and navy sets which unfortunately all had different, expensive blazers and inset V-neck colours and ties and hats. I hated all the hats.

'Didn't we go to school together?' asked a woman my age.
'Maybe. What colour uniform did we wear?'

Uniform Colour

I had to picture former students in appropriate coloured uniform to work out when I'd met them and where, or if later I'd been the teacher or visiting author to their school.

At the time, always 'being the new kid' at a school and having to make another group of friends seemed like a problem, but it turned out to be really good training for a writer. I learnt to observe, to work out people's motivations and to find out for myself how to survive even if I felt different.

Travelling on a country school bus was also an education.

When you arrive at a school mid-year, the friendships are already decided and there's a power structure. Only the very secure 'popular' kids, the 'kind ones' or the 'outsiders' are prepared to make friends with a newcomer. I was lucky in that I often made friends with the kind ones who took pity on me. Gaye was a dark skinned girl, who said she was part American Indian. I was intrigued by her exotic heritage. Decades later, I realised she was part Aboriginal, and wondered why she needed to keep that secret. She was a good friend to a newcomer and I appreciated her help.

When I went on the 2001 expedition to the Antarctic base of Casey Station, I was just as interested in the relationships and motivations of the highly skilled expeditioners, isolated in the ice from March through to November. This time, as writer, I was a professional observer of boffins and tradies who worked and lived together in the extreme Antarctic ice. I was intrigued to find a well-used copy of *Difficult Personalities* on the base. It's always weird to come across something written by yourself in an unexpected place and watch others reading it, not knowing that you were involved in the birth of that idea. A bit deflating when you find your autographed books dumped in Op Shops, but ...

Catching Up

Because secondary schools offered different subjects and languages, I was always trying to catch up. I started Form 1 at co-ed Gardiner Central (navy uniform) which was a selective 'feeder' school into Melbourne (for boys) and MacRobertson High (for girls) schools. You had to pass an entrance test, so most of the kids were quite competitive and my father was proud I qualified. I was more worried about whether I'd miss the bus and connecting tram at the transport hub and get there late on the first day. I always preferred trams to trains because you could get off and walk back if you found you were going in the wrong direction or overshot your stop because you were reading.

In that first term, we did Latin, and I enjoyed learning that language from an old, old woman with her hair scraped into a scraggly bun who loved words and whose name I've forgotten. My dad soon bought the Carrum Downs general store, and I started Term 2 at Frankston High (grey uniform) where they taught French. I was put in the lowest class and everybody mucked around. I was frustrated at the time-wasting but became friendly with Beverly, another keen student, who became my bridesmaid, much later.

My father had a major operation so I went to Camberwell High (green uniform) to live with my grandfather before we moved to Glengarry general store. I started at Traralgon High (grey uniform but different contrasting school colours) in Form 3, now known as Year 9, which I think was 1959, and stayed until 1961, before we moved back to the city. I finished Year 11 at Camberwell High (recycled green blazer), befriended again by kind schoolmate Rosy, and went to work in the State Bank because my family could not afford to keep me at school.

I learnt how to forge signatures, balance the tea-biscuit budget and mistakenly hit the bank-robber-holdup-under-counter-emergency-button with my knee while the accountant practised his golf swings out the back. The other female bank clerks taught me makeup, pop music and where to 'party'. A happy and kindly first workplace, but after my first year at Caulfield Tech night school, three evenings a week, studying accountancy and commercial law, I quit.

Why?

Informed that the bank only sponsored the study fees of male bank employees, as 'Females will just get married', I decided to finish the year of night school and leave the day job at the bank. 'Girls are not capable enough to become tellers, or be promoted.' I left, after getting a primary teaching place which required three years' payback in remote schools after graduation. Credited with my night class subjects despite failing at Accountancy, where the debit and credit columns confused me, I went to Toorak Teachers' college (just made it through Music—out of tune—and Chalkboard despite being unable to draw animals and decorate alphabetical borders on the blackboard). I then taught secondary English at Westall High, and became a teachers' college lecturer at Frankston and later a full-time author.

Traralgon High School

'Having to catch up' all the time meant I learnt how to research for myself—another useful skill for an author.

I can remember going to a careers day organised by Traralgon High, and we did psychology and IQ tests somewhere in the Latrobe Valley. I was disappointed to find that 'author' was not even suggested as a possible career in the boxes to be ticked. I always knew that's what I wanted to be, but I'd never met one personally.

Expectations were very different for boys. Girls were expected to marry the farmer (not become one), and teaching or nursing were regarded as the only options for 'clever' girls, but just as a fill-in until they married. I wanted to travel, and be a writer, so I decided not to get married, although I had boyfriends. Classes and subjects were streamed into 'academic', 'commercial' or 'technical'. If you could pass well, you were put in the academic stream with more maths and humanities and science subjects—university was the goal. If not, you did commercial with shorthand and typing and left as soon as possible, or you did art, woodwork, metalwork and mech drawing as technical. University was seen as top of the educational hierarchy and it cost lots of money to get there, so it wasn't an option unless you got a bursary of some kind, like teaching. Or had wealthy parents. I didn't.

In later life, I realised how limiting this streaming was. Working with 'tradies' in Antarctica, who had fantastic problem-solving and spatial skills, and having to use a computer keyboard as a six-finger hit-and-miss typist, I wished I'd had a broader education and been allowed to choose subjects across courses. After leaving school, you learn fast, because you can see the purpose of the skill. I had to do a search and rescue course for Antarctica. A vital skill, so you learn quickly. Formatting I never mastered.

Being Different as a Plus

I'm occasionally invited to speak at school reunions. Often the formerly 'popular', 'brainy' or 'physically able', who were the sporting heroes, prefects or school captains, have starred briefly during school days, but then declined into conformity. Surprisingly it's the 'runts' or the 'eccentric' kids, who were passionately interested in something outside the mainstream, who seem to have a more satisfying life later. Often they have been physically small, come from a cultural minority or split family, or had 'no money'. Finding ways of coping with these 'disadvantages' has given them the practice to cope with other challenges later in life. The other characteristic is encouragement from an enthusiastic teacher or mentor, or someone who has provided inspiration at a crucial stage.

As a writer, 'being different as a strength rather than a weakness' interests me greatly. A 'rich' life doesn't mean being 'a celebrity with millions', it means having the relationship and technical skills to construct a life and workstyle which is satisfying for you, and productive for the community. Plus a bit of fun. And a few adventures travelling in different countries or cultures.

As an author I've been lucky to interview people as diverse as a pyrotechnician (fireworks expert), helicopter pilot, funeral parlour embalmer, surveillance expert, oil-rig engineer, martial arts instructor, sniffer-dog–handler and a woman who releases celebratory doves at weddings. I've been able to 'see' through their eyes and share their experiences with readers of my books and articles.

At school, I was considered the quiet outsider, who was okay at netball, known as basketball then, who liked maths and who read a lot (even in the bath and the school bus) and was an observer. Being okay at sport was important in a country school, as social life revolved around weekend sporting events. I knew that. So I played the basketball position of defence in the school and Saturday community teams because I was tall. Female team matches were scheduled according to the boys' footy teams' fixtures, so we socialised, got lifts between the country ovals and 'hung out' at the Saturday night footy dance in the local Mechanics Institute in that small town on the fixture rotation. Everybody went to the footy dance, even your parents.

My first novel was called *General Store* and used the familiar setting of rural Gippsland but wasn't an autobiography. *Antarctic Writer on Ice* is as close to being autobiographical as I've written so far, and that was only because of circumstances of being beset in the polar ice, and some doubt about ever getting out. So the candid notes I e-mailed were widely read and eventually became the book which was published in Braille and audio too.

Being an author has been a quest for experiences in exotic and local places. One of the reasons I accepted the invitation to Traralgon High for Back to School Day was to share dreams. Maybe there are potential expeditioners, artists and cartographers here? Or occupations that don't have labels yet.

What do you genuinely like doing? Find work which involves you. Ignore the status or money.

Luck is a matter of preparation meeting opportunity.

Travel via translation in different cultures

CHAPTER 4
LITERARY SPEED DATING

Viewpoint

Viewpoint is an important technical decision. Should first person 'I' be used, which is more revealing than third person 'he' or 'she', and if so, is it really me or an assumed character?

Improvising in a workshop (to keep everybody awake after lunch), I suggested participant–historians became their most intriguing ancestor. They had to be interviewed, but stay in character, sustaining their ancestor role, and answer honestly, even if a murderer, bigamist or ex-con. The aim was to find out what descendants didn't know about their ancestor, and then research the missing facts.

This also works for fictional characters. I've seen child readers, dressed as their favourite fictional characters, interview the authors who had created them. Fascinating double viewpoints on creativity.

So here is speed-dating with the cake-eating hippo whom I created but on whose behalf I also reply. Questions are based on issues which intrigue readers but also retain the logic of fantasy. And all have been asked, and answered ambiguously by hippo, a.k.a. Hazel, across the past few years.

Q&A with Hippo Character Interviewing Author

I'm the cake-eating hippo who lives on Hazel's roof. Usually children read stories about me. NOW I can ask my author WHY, HOW and WHEN I happened.

Q: How old am I?

Hazel: The same age as the reader.

Q: How many candles will be on my next birthday cake?

Hazel: The right number to blow out.

Q: Where did you get the idea for me?

Hazel: Our new roof leaked. The workmen came to fix it. My then 4-year-old son Trevelyan said the noise was 'the hippo, eating cake on our roof'.

On another wet Saturday, my children and a neighbour Lani wrote their own hippo story and drew pictures.

Q: Real hippos eat carrots. I eat cake. Why?

Hazel: It's SPECIAL cake. There's an imagination muscle between your two ears. Exercise it to think of a special cake for you. Potato cake? Chocolate? Ice-cream? Cake of soap? Cup cake? Fish cake? You choose.

Q: Why do authors scribble on books?

Hazel: It's called autographing. When an author signs your book, it is special.

Q: What is the hippocampus? Is it where I live?

Hazel: Memories live in a special place in your brain. That's called the hippocampus. Authors often visit there.

Q: Who owns the book?

Hazel: The reader who uses the clues in the words and pictures to make their story.

Q: Each book has a different title. Was it hard to think of names for the books?

Hazel: As parents name children, authors have to name their books and their characters. Hippo is your name. Each hippo book-title starts with a different word, so librarians can find it in the catalogue.

Q: Hippopotamus is a hard word to spell. Hippo is shorter.

Hazel: Is that a question? Lots of children say Hittopotamus, and that's ok. That's why you have an H on your library bag, to help.

Q: Did you tell Deborah Niland how to draw me?

Hazel: No. But I did ask if the child could have jeans and a t-shirt and look like a boy or girl because it was an 'I' story. But Deborah drew a little girl.

Q: How did you know I was a 'he'?

Hazel: Readers decided. And we even had a competition to name the baby. Amus was one suggestion (it means friend). And it's in the word HippopotAMUS.

Q: What do you say when children knock at your door and ask, 'Is this the house where the hippo lives?'

Hazel: Have a look.

Q: Did I go to Cake-School?

Hazel: Yes. You are a Master Chef. You are good at stirring. You know the recipe for a book. Slurps of fun. Dashes of jokes. Litres of laughing. And a big friend with all the answers.

Q: What is my favourite dance?

Hazel: You can belly-dance really well. But cake-walking is your best dance. That's a joyful strut on the roof.

Q: Do I still live in the same place?

Hazel: Yes. Except when you go on holiday. Or to hospital. Or to the playground. Or the other places in the books.

Q: When my picture books are drawn, which page is done first?

Hazel: The illustrator decides. Sometimes it's the cover.

Q: Which picture do you like best?

Hazel: Playing hide and seek on the roof, with just a little bit of you showing. Some think it's your elbow.

Q: Is it?

Hazel: Depends what the reader thinks.

Q: If my story is in another language, can I read the translation?

Hazel: You might enjoy 'feeling' the Braille copy. Or working out the words in Chinese, or signing in Auslan.

Q: What else can I do on the roof?

Hazel: Anything. Children often send their pictures of you playing 'sokker'. Or riding a bike. Or playing hide and seek.

Q: Are you good at spelling big words like Hittopotamus?

Hazel: I try.

Q: Do you ever get things wrong?

Hazel: Yes. The best stories come from things going wrong. Or embarrassing moments, like standing with you under the Over-Sized Baggage sign at the airport.

Q: How many drafts do you write of my stories?

Hazel: At least ten.

Q: How long does it take to write a Hippo picture book?

Hazel: There is thinking time. Then there is writing time. And re-writing time. And then it takes about a year for the illustrations.

Q: Why have I got three toes?

Hazel: Because you're special.

Q: Can my toes fit on the keyboard?

Hazel: Sometimes. Other times, I write answers to fan mail for you.

Q: If I'm the character and you're the author, who knows more about me?

Hazel: Who do you think?

Q: What are the best questions children have asked you about me, the cake-eating hippo?

Hazel: I'll share some. I answer fan mail for you occasionally.
   I explain that I am writing on behalf of Hippo, as his feet don't fit on the keyboard.

Q1. I haven't got a friend. Will you come and sit on my roof?

A1. Yes. If you invite me.

Q2. My mum went to Weight Watchers to lose weight. Don't you think you should stop eating so much cake?

A2. I also eat fish cakes and rice cakes.

Q3. Do you talk?

A3. Only to those who listen.

Q4. Did your bum get sunburnt when you didn't fit under the umbrella?

A4. You can check the illustration in the book.

Q5. When they put on the seatbelts, there were three clicks and four people, why?

A5. Maybe two clicked at once? Three of anything always works better in a story.

Q6. What's the name of the baby? Is it a boy or a girl?

A6. What do you think? One reader thought it was called 'Just Right'.

Q7. I went to hospital in an ambulance. But there was no hippo on the roof of mine. Where were you?

A7. I was directing traffic. At the hospital, I was telling doctors what to do.

Q8. Why aren't you in the holiday photos?

A8. I'm shy. I don't always fit in.

Q9. Do you play soccer on the roof? I like soccer best.

A9. I play football ... It could be Aussie Rules, rugby union or league or gridiron. D'you think it looks like soccer? I play all positions. Even referee and umpire.

Q10. Can you read in different languages when your book is translated? Is there a hippo-speak? Hippo language?

A10. Yes. I understand everything. I belong to everybody.

The answer is yes to the next questions.

Q. In the hospital, did they put a band aid on the sore bit?

Yes.

Q. My book is worn out. Can I get one the same?

Yes.

Q. Will I ever meet your other characters from other books?

Yes.

Hazel: I've answered your questions Hippo. May I ask you one? What happens after the end of the book?

Hippo: We read it again, together.

CHAPTER 5
THE PLATEAU OF BOREDOM

The Process of Creativity: Or the Writer's Block You're Not Having!

Creativity is a map. I have to reach a plateau of boredom, a feeling that everything is flat and monotonous. To avoid the 'nothing-ness', I put two things together that have never been in that combination before, which become a new idea for a story.

To avoid being stuck on that plateau forever, I write an alternative mental world which provides the terrain of variety. Rivers of thoughts. Occasional peaks. Rocky stretches of plotting when I have to find alternative routes. And glimpses of characters. (Now I could have added 'in the fog' but that would have been too predictable and stretching the analogy.)

This morning I woke up with that map image. I hadn't thought of creativity quite in that way before. Early mornings are when I have my best ideas, before the minutia of domesticity takes over. Ideally a couple of hours at the computer keyboard to capture the elusive early ideas before having to shower, make breakfast, and travel to work. That's why, when my children were younger, I did my best snatched writing before they woke or when I was away alone in motels on author tours. But in real life, I take early minutes at the keyboard and am grateful that my Skype does not have a web cam on automatically, so the occasional caller cannot see what I am not wearing.

On reflection, perhaps weekly family orienteering on Sundays provided the map image. Trying to find an elusive control on a bush map when you're tired, knowing it's there somewhere, but you have to stop, and rest for a moment. (I often looked at the local wildlife like passing 'roos for inspiration, as they always seem to know where they're loping.) And then I'd go back and try to find the route, like plotting a novel.

Using an existing map is one challenge. Creating the map is another.

Creating the map

> This morning I'm grateful, because I have a prospective title: *The Map of Serendipity*. The contradiction in terms appeals because a map is planned with co-ordinates and verifiable directions. Serendipity is when pleasant coincidences occur (as well as Serendip being the original name for Sri Lanka, a piece of trivia that doesn't really fit this concept). Serendip is the faculty of finding valuable or agreeable things not sought for. While driving I listen to audio books and recently was inspired by crime writer P.D. James's memoir of a year of her creativity when she was in her late seventies. It contained flashbacks, but wasn't a boredom of chronology. That's the country of the mind I would like to visit and re-visit. So in this coming year, I want to explore my idiosyncratic version of the process of creativity.

Googling 'Serendip' provides this:

> A word coined by Horace Walpole, who says that he had formed it upon the title of the fairy-tale *The Three Princes of Serendip*, the heroes of which 'were always making discoveries, by accidents and sagacity, of things they were not in quest of'.

That is not relevant to my ideas quest, and I mustn't go down that route, especially as I'm a skeptic more interested in hippocampus processes than beings from other worlds. Being seduced into idea byways when researching is a dead end for a professional writer. Fascinating, but it's necessary to return to the major project and maybe store that item on the computer under the 'Follow Up Later' file.

As a published writer since my late twenties, I'm beginning to recognise the pattern of creativity in my workstyle. After a busy period finishing multiple projects, I seem to have a barren, flat time, when I don't think that I will write any more. Can't see the point. I turn my attention to 'administrivia' or 'things that I ought to do'. When I'm on this plateau, I don't recognise it as fatigue. There will be an overheard phrase, often from a child ('Does water have bones?'), a sign like DEAD END and ONE WAY ONLY beside the cemetery. The juxtaposing of ideas, a visit to a setting which has mysterious potential, and then there's a slight interest awakening in how this might be captured in words.

One Way Only

I don't believe in the concept of writer's block. I think it is a self-indulgence by those unwilling to discipline themselves. Routine writing can be produced to a deadline by a disciplined professional and the quality will be acceptable. That is adequate, but not euphoric.

What I am trying to convey by 'creativity' is the serendipitous pleasure or the joy when an idea is charted. When something that wasn't there before is begun, and shaped to be shared, and the experience is genuine, not routine.

Re-creation occurs on the page or screen when the writer's carefully chosen and positioned words re-create an approximation in the mind of the reader of that first, significant experience.

The cake-eating hippo on the roof is an example of creation, of juxtaposing unlikely ideas which symbolise reassurance and with which the reader can identify. And the 'hippocampus' idea, which is a real part of the brain, can be linked to the thought processes. That is a possibility.

I am content with a 1000 rough but usable words for my early morning concept of a map paralleling the creative process. And maybe the title of Hippocampus? As a colony of the mind? Or an outpost? Certainly not populated by People of the Platitudes. How about *Let Hippos Eat Cake* as a working title? But that doesn't fit the symbol of the map.

Need to delete that! What you leave out can be an equally important decision in the process of creativity.

The real Shire of Bland, paired with the overseas town of Boring. Hazel was part of a wonderful non-boring Literary Festival at Condobolin in that shire.

CHAPTER 6
STORY STEALING

Do Authors Steal Others' Stories?

'Steal' implies theft. I prefer to call it recycling. Yes, authors do collect the quirky or embarrassing moments and re-use or exaggerate in stories, sometimes calling the result fiction. Just distilled moments of angst. Others label it tall stories, research, or income for lawyers.

What have I stolen recently?

Naughtiest Pets from a newspaper contest: the dog who ate winning ticket worth $5000, the puppy who chewed guest's boot under dinner table so that guest left with less than a pair of boots. Or the nibbling goat who punctured the swimming pool, which flooded the backyard. Not forgetting the family pet which ate Dad's wallet with all the credit cards. But in fiction, you'd concentrate all embarrassing habits into the one pet character.

Casual airport or train conversations with strangers often provide an unusual angle or mini-story. But then the writer goes further with a twist of 'What if?' Talking with a truck driver who loved motor bikes:

What if the Harley Davidson bikie was a hi-tech chook, who could mind-read?

What if, on the day of her Gran's funeral, Zoe discovers her grandmother had fake ID for years?

Often I transfer a family idea to a different setting.

Mystery Twin was inspired by a real family with an older brother and cute, much younger twin sisters who got all the attention. So the older brother invented a Super Twin for himself who could do anything, and he then had to be both people. I transferred the setting to a cruise ship (on which we'd travelled as a family for a fortnight and I wrote onboard) and made it a mystery to provide tension and humour. The final characters didn't physically look like the real Asian family. The names and personalities were different but the motivation of being jealous leading to creative problem-solving was real, even if fiction.

Youthful readers prefer characters their age or slightly older.

So although I heard the anecdote about an adult betraying a family secret, and put it in my ideas notebook, I'd have to plot so that betraying a family secret is relevant for the child character.

What if an old woman with dementia tells a family 'secret' hidden for decades, which has criminal, financial or genetic implications? 'Gran mixed up my Dad and her ex-husband.' In what way might this be relevant for an 11-year-old?

Character traits I collect from real life, and then 'play around' with them, to fit my fictional personalities. Sometimes human foibles are given to animals or insects, like my clumsy Bumble from *Flight of the Bumblebee* or director duck with attitude from *Stickybill* who tells everybody what to do. Embarrassing moments often end up in later, published stories. But what if three authors share the same experience? Who owns the anecdote? Is it an ethical problem of who owns what when all wish to write about it?

TAPS (Think, Act, Publicise) is the trio of authors who help each other. We are not three drips, as is often joked.

Who OWNS the Fishy Tale?

Individually, our trio of authors had been invited to speak at a library conference at the Wrest Point Casino in bayside Hobart in Tasmania. Since Margaret Clark was our VIP author, she had an inside hotel room, with a fridge which later became strategic in the Great Salmon Fiasco! Author Krista Bell and I were in a cheaper shared apartment—an extreme, hilly walking distance away. We all became intimately involved in a fishy business ... The red herring of a large and embarrassing salmon which had to be hidden, and then we all had an interest in using the embarrassing story later.

The husband of a colleague had visited Snug Butchery, a local Tasmanian smoked salmon shop, in the company of some gourmet food writers who enthused about the quality and offered to buy at a bulk discount for any interested authors.

He turned up at 9 a.m. on Conference Day 1 with three BIG salmon which had to be kept cool. The hotel kitchen refrigerator was locked, and only Margaret had an in-house bar fridge, but she was speaking on the platform. Publisher Jill Morris offered the temporary loan of her bar fridge and keys were exchanged. Hazel and Krista were unable to collect the fish later that afternoon because when they knocked, Jill and her husband were having a nap.

Day 2, 9 a.m. Jill returned the salmon as she was checking out. Presenter Hazel slipped it between her lecture notes until it could be placed in Margaret's fridge. So the dead salmon heard a literary talk about Writing Humour and was present on a panel about Fact & Fiction. In between, it was frequently checked and jokes made about Hazel's perfume. That night, due to rowdy neighbours, Margaret impulsively changed rooms to a quieter corridor, forgot her fridge resident and left the salmon behind.

Day 3. As temporary Custodian of the Salmon, Margaret remembered she'd left it in the hotel fridge on check-out day. A mad dash to Reception to get the key, a mad dash up to her room, a heart-stopping moment when she saw that the room had been cleaned and bed made, a worse heart-stopping moment when she opened the fridge! Phew, as in relief, not bad smell. It was still there! Then a mad dash through bemused hotel pokies players with Hazel clutching The Salmon.

The Salmon then attended several lectures, poking out of Hazel's red shoulder bag.

Krista carried her salmon in her arms like a baby until hotel staff took pity and offered their cool store. Going through Hobart customs, behind a Pop musical group, Hazel's luggage was closely checked too and smelled by airport staff but the Salmon was passed and later eaten.

101 Uses for a Handbag

Each of the writers agreed to use their own versions in subsequent stories. Look out for 'The Great Salmon Fiasco', 'Fishy Business' and '101 Uses for a Handbag.'

And if you're invited to drinks and nibbles with any of these writers, check out the history of the Salmon which has another 'airing'.

Shared at Alice Springs 'Writers in the Centre' Festival where Authors' Embarrassing Moments were after-dinner entertainment. Lots of applause and a standing ovation. No fish was served on the menu that night.

Some stories you never steal, even if tempted. Those belonging to mentorees or children in your writing workshops. Litigious non-writers. Secrets from your own family. Which ones? Can't tell.

Margaret Clark, Krista Bell & Hazel

CHAPTER 7
GENERAL STORE

Cobwebs of Ideas

Did people or books influence you most as a teenager?

People influenced me more than books.

My grandfather had a private Lending Library in the front room of his house, and because I'd finished the Children's Section by the time I was 10, which was mainly Enid Blyton, I started reading adult books. He guided me in the direction of Espionage, Mystery and Biography, which were on the lower shelves, rather than Westerns and Romance. The only book I remember by name was *The Land of Far Beyond* which was Enid Blyton's version of *Pilgrim's Progress*, a kind of Quest. Journeys or the quest shape for a story is a common structure. Our son now has Quest as a middle name. I love Q names, especially if you have a boring surname like Edwards. My computer is called Quentin.

Where did you go to primary school?

Ashburton Primary. But I lived at the grandly named 75 Victory Boulevard, Alamein, a post WW2 Housing Commission estate where all the new streets had historic battle names. My father was proud to own his own small home, as housing was in short supply, and our garden was immaculate with flowers, vegetables and a silver fence he built. He also converted the back shed into my 'cubby' with a window, and wooden floor. That 'cubby' was the envy of local kids for whom it became play HQ. Early Sunday morning, I nearly burnt down the cubby while illegally toasting marshmallows over a naked flame for the neighbourhood gang. My grandparents lived next door to Ashburton Primary a kilometre away, and I stayed with them before and after school.

How did living in a General Store help your writing?

General Store was the Australian name for a country store in a small township.
When I was 14, wanting to be an author and being a readaholic was not common. I didn't know any authors personally until I was 23. Most of the books I read had English or European backgrounds.
Serving in a country general store in the 1950s was good training for a would-be writer. Customers of all kinds, rude and polite. I read every newspaper and magazine and I folded it up again properly for re-sale. I ate ice creams or lollies whenever I liked.
I lived in a house attached to a general store in Gippsland for two years. Previously our family worked in a smaller store for two years, so we lived on the job in both places. We didn't have a car. Or a TV. But I did listen to radio serials. Open 7 a.m. until 9 p.m. seven days a week, we sold everything.
Our store was a newsagency, a bank, and a 'corner grocery store'. We also sold hardware supplies like nails, paint and glue. Although it was not a garage, the store sold petrol and oil. Farmers would come in once a week for their food orders. They'd leave squiggly lists, or say, 'The usual'. Then I'd have to work out what they wanted.
Once I put in a tube of 'fastglue' instead of 'toothpaste'. One customer had 'sticky' teeth that night!
Before and after school and on weekends, I served in the shop. In busy times, a girl helped, but most days it was just Dad, Mum and me. I was an only child.
I learnt to mix up milkshakes and make 'spiders' (lemonade, ice cream and flavouring with a straw). I hand-pumped petrol.

You had to pull and push the pump handle on the old petrol bowser. On the scales, I weighed and bagged sugar, pollard and bran. Once, using the big meat slicer, I nearly sliced my hand instead of the ham.

I still remember the general store smell of 'mixed-up' food and fuel. It was special, spicy and yet disinfected.

When we first moved in, names were a problem. Country people often share surnames. Some even look like each other. And they expected us to know who was who.

To help, Dad kept a little name-book.

'And exactly how do you spell your name?' he'd say politely.

'B.I.L.L. S.M.I.T.H.' laughed the farmer.

All the customers smiled. So did Dad.

King, Lang and Friend were the most common names. Getting the names right was important, especially for newcomers. And you were considered a newcomer for about 20 years.

At 6 a.m. the train whistle blew. The guard threw out the newspapers. Dad collected the bundle from the railway station.

'Regulars' would have their surnames written on their newspapers. Dad had beautiful copperplate handwriting. 'Orders' were on one table. Extra newspapers were for sale on the other table. Frequently, a family with the same name would take the wrong paper, or 'casual' customers would pick up orders—then there was a fuss. Dad started to write their initials or first names as well, so they'd pick the right one. His special pen was inky.

Many people had first names starting with A. I liked seeing A. King, A. Farmer or A. Friend. That's when I decided NEVER to give my child a name starting with A. Imagine being A. Fool!

We didn't have television, so newspapers were important. Customers got cross if another family had taken 'their paper'.

Sometimes I'd pretend that Dad's inky writing of an A was really an R and give them their relatives' paper. Then I'd keep my fingers crossed that the other family didn't come in when I was 'on duty'.

Our family meals were eaten in 'shifts', because someone

had to be 'on' in the shop. Since I had some meals by myself, I started the bad habit of read-eating.

Reading let me escape into other worlds. In between customers, I was supposed to stack shelves. Instead I read all the magazines, books and newspapers.

Each afternoon, Jo the part-time mailman left on his 'mail-run' after a detour to the pub for lunch and a few drinks. He delivered letters to farmers' roadside mailboxes. He also took our uncollected orders. If it rained, the inky names ran on the newspapers.

I listened to customers' stories. In a small country town, the general store is the 'gossip centre'. We heard everything first. 'Serving' meant learning to speak to people of all ages. I learnt to control nuisances and to challenge shoplifters. I also learnt how to say 'No,' when people asked for credit, but my father often helped families who were having a hard time. That was part of the reason we eventually went broke ourselves; people didn't pay their bills.

Glengarry General Store

I got lots of practice working out change, adding up orders and 'doing the books'. So maths was easy for me.

In an emergency, people used our phone. So I learnt about 'a baby coming', road or farm accidents and even floods.

I especially remember the bushfires. In a country town, everybody belonged to the Country Fire Authority. C.F.A.

In summer, when the fire-bell or siren went, so did you! Neighbours always helped. Next time it could be your place in the path of the fire.

Because we had the store, Dad gave free petrol, drinks and sandwiches to the fire-fighters. Often I would take drink crates out to the fire. I remember the smell of burning bush, smoke and the sweaty fire-fighters. Once the smoke drifted across our general store. That was a worry because of our petrol tank. The good news was that the fire-fighters turned the fire in time.

On the Monday after the fire, one grumpy customer complained that his newspaper was missing. I knew why. There were photos of the fire-fighters in the newspaper. Everybody wanted a picture of themselves. We ran out of papers that day.

Gossip

'News' and 'gossip' were swapped at dances too.

At the Saturday night 'footy' dances at the Mechanics Hall, Dad got me up for the Barn Dance, where you change partners in a circle. At that time, it wasn't 'nerdy' to dance with your father in that sort of place. But I still felt embarrassed. Lacking a sense of rhythm, I've never been much good at dancing. But in the Barn Dance you move onto the next partner fairly quickly, and they forget you trod on their toes.

Then they had the Mexican Hat Dance. You jump up and down, in time to the band. Unluckily, it was a very old hall. Everybody jumped heavily. The band played. Dad swung me around.

Crash!

The dance floor fell in.

Too many, heavy dancers!

That's when I decided I wouldn't be a dancer. I'd be a writer.

Next day, in the local newspaper, there was a picture of the broken dance hall. But we didn't run out of newspapers that day. Dad ordered extra.

My father was different. He'd read books like: The Rhubiyat of Omar Kyam, Robbie Burns poetry or 'The Writings of Marcus Aurelius'. My reading was never censored, but he'd ask embarrassing questions in front of my friends like Why, How or When?

Sometimes school friends would stop overnight. They loved 'serving' in the shop. They loved making double-header ice-creams or milkshakes.

The Socratic Method

Dad would show them how to work the milkshake machine. He'd say, 'Why do you think it works like this?' My friends didn't know. Neither did I. But I knew asking questions was his habit.

He'd keep asking until I worked out answers.

Only later, when studying to be a teacher, did I learn that it was called The Socratic Method, asking questions until the listener worked out personal answers.

He taught me it was okay to be different. Or to ask questions if you didn't know things. A writer needs to notice things. And in a country town, we were the 'new' outsiders. We hadn't been born there. He said being an outsider was often the best way to see more.

He would say, 'Yes, why not?' to climbing a high tree, going in a speedboat or riding a horse. Other parents said, 'No. It's too dangerous.'

When I did my homework behind the counter at night, Dad was interested. He loved maths puzzles. When I brought maths problems home, he'd do them too. My maths homework was regarded as fun, by him, not me until he explained that maths and music were just other languages for different kinds of ideas. But I didn't speak music well.

I loved reading, especially by torch-light under my blankets, but one place I didn't read was the country toilet. In those days, the 'night-man' changed the can once a week. And despite the strongly smelling flowers growing around the outside 'dunny', I hated the smell. And the cobwebs.

Old newspapers were cut in squares and used as toilet paper in some 'dunnies'.

Inky print left marks. This didn't happen in ours. We sold toilet rolls in the store.

And we used proper toilet paper outside. No way was I having an inky name on me.

Alternatively the cobwebs were like idea-threads for stories, and I could think about them.

However, after two years in that general store, we went back to the city. There was one good thing about that. A Toilet! An inside toilet. No cobwebs. And no old newspapers with inky words that came off on your ... fingers.

Perhaps that's why I prefer ironic rather than toilet humour in my stories now? My first published novel was *General Store*, where only the setting was autobiographical. Some people thought 'General' was a military rank and Store was the surname so it wasn't a good title. And translated into Finnish, it was the equivalent of Josie's Store which was probably a better title even if I didn't speak Finnish. That's when I began to realise that a book could travel, even further than the author, and into other cultures.

17-year-old Hazel

CHAPTER 8
FAN MAIL

Fans

'Cake-eating Hippo is my best friend', tweeted a fan on National Best Friends' Day on August 15th.

'R. U. a book teacher?' was a query about the author's job.

Sometimes the fan mail is addressed to my character.

'Dear Hippo, I haven't got a friend. Will you come and sit on my roof?'

That's when I have to write back 'in character'. These days it's more likely to be e-mail, so all my characters are only as digital as me. Not sure how the cake-eating Hippo gets his toes on the keyboard, but he does. And I also have a literate duck companion in my study. And the hundreds and thousands girl who figures people in the shape of numbers. Frequently asked questions (FAQs) with answers are on my website to save time for students doing projects, but original questions keep coming.

'Dear Stickybeak, where were you before you were a duck?'

'I was an egg, and before that, I was an idea.'

So glad this was not a face-to-face question and there was time to compose an e-mail answer. At a group storytelling, I would say, 'What a good question,' to gain time to think of an appropriate answer.

Web chats require fast responses, as viewers can see you on screen, and your working mess behind. Occasionally I move the camera around to show what my study really looks like. I treasured this compliment from an early Territory Tales web chat during Literacy and Numeracy Week, at a time when we were all experimenting electronically and often conversations 'fell out' due to outback connections, or the lack of them.

'You've got a lot of books in your study. We can see them.'

'Hi Hazel; Us mob think you are a good author because you have good books that make us happy. From Gus, Dontay & Vernon Katherine South Primary School.'

One New Zealand big conference link-up had lighting problems as I was in the 7 a.m. dark of Melbourne and they were two hours later, and the choice was either I saw them or they saw me. We had to close the blind slats in my study for lighting continuity so I was talking in the dark, unable to see notes, across the hour session as the sun rose and the light changed my end, but they could see giant me on their conference screen. Occasionally I could hear a laugh, but it was very difficult to judge audience response.

I get nervous dealing with new technology, and it can be exhausting when you're unsure if the connections will work and apprehensive knowing you lack the skill to fix problems online or understand 'techie' verbs like 'export' or 'import'. Answering through an interpreter on a web chat with Nanjing, China was extra challenging. We had audio fall out and delays but also had to allow for the cultural courtesies of what was considered polite to ask of an author writing in English. Hard to evaluate whether pauses are technical flaws or lack of interest.

So the choice is either to drive to a professional studio, adding travel time and parking at weird hours, or to speak from home. My solution was to learn just enough technology to use my own computer link-up. And deal with the apprehension.

A 4 a.m. chat (my Melbourne time) with an American school took 15 minutes and then I went back to bed. But you have to check your maths about the time zones and query whether they mean 10 a.m. their time or yours. I once miscalculated an hour on daylight saving summer time.

Nanjing International Cultural Educational delegation

International School, Balikpapan, Indonesia.

Dolly Parton Charity 'Imagination library' visit. Ballarat.

Talkback radio attracts great questions. So do author ambassador visits, especially related to literacy charities like singer Dolly Parton's 'Imagination Library'. Dolly's practical help for impoverished kids who can't read is highly valued. She came from poor circumstances and hasn't forgotten that, so quality books are distributed to pre-schoolers free, and her business skills support the donations.

In addition, I offer a personally signed book for the most imaginative question from the group. This was encouragement in a regional area where some children were not familiar even with the concept of a question. So I told them about the 'imagination muscles' between their two ears which needed exercise.

'Use your imagination muscle.'

I suggested like footy training, asking questions was 'warming up' exercises for your brain.

The teacher helped them prepare some written questions. One boy asked, 'How did the hippo get on the roof?'

I replied, 'What do you think?'

There was a long silence. One of those times when you need to wait.

I made a few suggestions. 'A ladder? Parachute? A giant jump on the trampoline?'

He shook his head and you could see the concentration. He was really thinking. 'A jet pack!'

His teacher was in tears. Usually this 8-ish-year-old boy did not become involved in class.

Executive decision. His was the most imaginative question.

Later I autographed his book, and unprompted he thanked me.

'This is my first book, ever. We don't have books at our place.'

'Will you promise me to read a page tonight?'

'Yeah. I might.'

Another discussion strategy is to give the answer, and ask them to make up a question.

'If the answer is purple, what is the question?'

Many will say 'What do red and blue make?', but others will play with ideas like the child who said, 'If you like red but you get the blues sometimes.'

'If the answer is a book, what is the question?' is a great discussion starter.

Always enjoyed describing myself as a 'problem writer' and loved 'judging' how imaginative minds worked together. I used to create original problems for the Tournament of Minds contest started by two innovative educators Pam Russell and Ev Tindale. These scenarios were open-ended plots, where students came up with solutions, often better than any I envisaged, and then performed the scenario, within time and space limits, on Tournament Day as a group of problem-solvers with maths, engineering, language or social issues. A Queensland country town team starred at Tournament of Minds annually due to one encouraging teacher, and years later I noticed their tourist initiatives to bring people to their town and wondered if the ex-child problem-solvers had now grown up. If so, one innovative teacher had made a difference to Dalby's economic future. Intellectual capital which repaid the investment.

Hippocampus:

My favourite age of the mind is four because they play with fantastic possibilities.

I love four-year-old minds which are intrigued by concepts such as time and geography.

'Half past Grandma,' was one four-year-old's explanation of where you could buy beach clothes like those in *My Hippopotamus is on our Caravan Roof Getting Sunburnt*. Grandma's was obviously a location associated with beaches and sand.

Or 'last week' being the explanation of anything in the past and 'tomorrow' being any time in the future.

'I was in my Mummy's tummy. I knocked three times when I was ready to come out.' Now that's an imaginative viewpoint of the creation process. And the kind of phrase I'd capture in my ideas notebook for a story 'tomorrow'.

Authors need to listen for the new kinds of child logic and viewpoints.

Four-year-old: 'Do cars have bones?'
Adult: 'Sort of, but not like human bones.'
Four-year-old: 'Not like human bones?'
(Silence)
Four-year-old: 'Does water have bones?'

I am a fan of this thinking. If encouraged, they will become our adult problem-solvers who build bridges and new worlds.

They'll be prepared to take 'risk' and get it wrong occasionally.

But if discouraged by too many rules and fearful of making a mistake, that potential is lost to us all.

Part of the reason for the hippo's popularity is that he is the imaginary friend, which many children need and create. A bigger friend with all the answers to deal with the unknown.

'I'm four. What number are you?'
'Sixty-eight.'
'Next birthday I'll have green candles on my birthday cake.'
'Why?'
'Because I'll be a boy. Boys like blue or green.'
'I'm a girl. I like green too.'
'I used to be a girl.'
'When?'
'Last week. I was number 3. Last birthday.'
'What colour were your candles then?'
'Pink. Girls like pink.'
'I'm a girl. I like purple.'
'Some girls like pink AND purple,' was the kindly response.
'How do you know you're a boy now? Is Daddy a boy?'
'Yes. But next birthday he'll be a girl.'
'What about YOUR next birthday ...?'
'You take turns. I'll be a girl.'
'If you're not a boy or a girl what are you?
'An Alien,' said the 6-year-old brother.

A question mark rainbow candle may be the answer. Recycled.

Adult fan queries to authors are different. Often they don't write unless they have a complaint, need advice or wish to query a fact. Co-written with Dr Helen McGrath, our factual *Difficult Personalities* has provoked many callers on radio talkback plus others via e-mail. Almost ten times the number for our *Friends* book. Not sure if that indicates difficult personalities outnumber friends? Or that sociopaths are a more fascinating subject?

Decades after *General Store* was released, but just after a *Country Life* magazine feature mentioned my first novel set in

Gippsland, a woman queried the flowers around the outdoor dunny. She claimed her grandmother had lived in the same 'real' general store, and had planted those flowers. She wanted to get a copy of the out-of-print *General Store* novel but it was too expensive online in the rare books section. Could I send her one. I explained that it was a novel but I'd drawn on the real setting and we agreed that maybe her gran had lived there.

Fiction writers have to be careful about writing 'close to home' and 'dramatic licence' but I've never been sued nor pulped.

Outback Ferals fan query.

'Did you mean the threatened pandemic of feral pigs were the outback ferals or did you mean the people who live in the outback like in Darwin?'

'Which do you think?'

The title of this novel is deliberately ambiguous. And Young Adult (Y.A.) is a thoughtful readership where story matters and issues can be explored in depth not always possible in adult fiction. The age of YA readers is elastic and they follow a character or an author. And with a new group of readers each generation, which is about six years, these novels have a longer life.

Fan Art

My *f2m: the boy within* co-author Ryan got lots of e-fan mail. Even fan art.

'This book saved my life. Others have coped with the same as me.'

Fan art often includes parodies where the format and wording of the original book is followed but with new content. Sort of legal piracy but as a compliment. So the hippo is a favourite for structure and rhythm but also for students of any age learning to read, especially in English as a second language.

Poignant

Intended checking my various files to find the most poignant fan mail, but then I decided to write from memory. Certain readers stay with you.

I'm unsure why the big, primary-coloured illustrations often comfort sick children, but they do.

Cake-Angels connected to the Ronald McDonald House donated a special hippo cake for patients and their families when I shared stories. Cake-Angels are cake shops or individual cake decorators who donate their skills to create one-off cakes with themes relevant to the interests of individual sick children. Trains. Super heroes. Fairy pink. Clowns. Football. Often these children and their siblings have long-term associations with hospitals, and fantasy can help draw them into other worlds, away from the pain and sometimes the boredom of routine medical procedures.

The most poignant would be B, a much loved but incapacitated 13-year-old, for whom 'Hippo' was her favourite, read-daily, multiple-times book. I didn't know of B until after her funeral at which the book was read. Told of this at a literary festival some months later, by an illustrator colleague who was her family friend, I found a gift copy in my briefcase of *Guess What? There's a Hippopotamus on the Hospital Roof Eating Cake*, but was unsure what to write as the dedication. After some thought, I autographed it to the family of B.

A private Facebook message arrived unexpectedly.

> Dear Hazel, you don't know me, but recently you gave a copy of one of your books to my daughter via F. who told you about B and her recent passing. B loved your books; all of them, but the hospital one was particularly her favourite, maybe because she knew the journey in the ambulance so well herself! She shredded many copies and got at least 1 new hippopotamus book a

year! I went so far as to record them for her with me telling the story so she could read them off my iPhone when we were out and she was bored! She was and is our angel. Blessings to you, from B and her family.

While checking the family's permission to use this anecdote, her mother said 'Yes. What a wonderful gift. Today would have been B's birthday!' Poignant.

Another parent, who read *Guess What? There's a Hippopotamus on the Hospital Roof Eating Cake* en route in the ambulance to calm the child, then sent me a thank-you note. This was a memorable example of bibliotherapy, of using books for emotional reasons—as distractors.

Other fanciful questions to hippo are fun to answer.

> I was wondering, what do you do when you run out of cake? And what are your favourite hobbies?
> Abby, Age 9

> I might take cooking lessons. My hobbies are swimming in mud and reading about hippo cousins.

Often whole classes claim there's a hippo on their roof and send personal drawings of extremely creative activities like 'playing sokker', losing library books or riding dirt bikes across the roof tiles.

'How To ...' books provoke different kinds of fan mail because many are seeking strategic answers. Grateful families give *Writing a Non-Boring Family History* to elderly relatives to encourage 'anecdultery' rather than shipping lists of begats, births, deaths and marriages.

Authors are often contacted as a last resort for their out-of-print books. My early adult literacy *Workdays* series was based on real people explaining a day in their life. Coy about her real age, 'Rita the Customs Officer' suggested 'middle aged' rather than a specific age for her bio facts. This year her neighbour contacted me for a hard-to-find copy of the decades old book to celebrate Rita's 80th after she returned from her voyage to Alaska. What a subject Rita turned out to be. She invited me to afternoon tea, on her return from icy Alaska. And now I can calculate how old she was at the original interview. Ageless.

Corridor of Characters

'Corridor' was a national touring exhibition of children's fan letters and illustrations to my characters and the responses (written by me in character). Easy to mount and exhibit either side of a corridor, it was also meant to be corridors of the mind where characters lived. Mainly shown in libraries and galleries, the most intriguing venue was the ex-Fremantle maximum security jail, now Literature Centre.

Legally letters belong to the letter writer, not the author recipient, and many children were a bit careless about contact details which meant some could not be included. Others were thrilled to be involved.

My favourite was: 'How many ruff coppies do you do? I need this last week.' No return edress or address.

My favourite adult question was: How many hippo miles/ kilometres have you travelled?

Answer. Does that include air travel? Stopped counting.

Witty Women Lunches

Started when a misguided male said there were no witty women, twenty-five acquaintances were invited to bring a themed plate of food to share and a quote by or about a witty woman. This developed into an annual event with themes like witty women of Music, Hat-tricks (with passions on the hat), Adventure, Spirited or Science. All guests complained but loved to come. It was agreed that 'Blue' was the worst theme for catering and now we all know why chefs use blue Band-Aids (show up because there is little blue food).

Illustrator Felicity Marshall digitally enhanced me informing us that a filbert is a 'Cultured Hazelnut'. Then sang her parody to fit the Music theme. Extract below.

> **The Hazel Days**
>
> She's a paperback writer
> She'll get that text tighter
> She's been to Antarctica
> Had a weird virus called Galactica
> Belly dancing so groovy
> Go shake that booty
> And rock on, rock on
> Rock on through the Hazel days
>
> © Felicity Marshall 2011

And then came the portraits.

Di Keating's 'Hippo-pot-a-musing' was entered in the 1999 Archibald Prize. The clouds represented the book characters and the letters were the as-yet-unwritten stories. Twenty hours of sitting and NOT talking. 'Lilac Haze' was painted from a magazine cover photo by Anne Cunningham. Unfortunately this made it ineligible for some portrait contests, despite Anne respecting copyright permissions. Eligible portraits have to be painted from life, not a photo. Weird to have multiples of yourself in a household but fabulous experience to watch the hands of visual artists creating.

NOT JUST A PIECE OF CAKE · BEING AN AUTHOR

f2m doco film crew at Kailash Studio.

Fan art by Rooster Tails   A 'Filbert' or 'Philbert' is a cultured hazelnut

Di Keating's Archibald entry 'Hippopotamusing'

'Lilac Haze' by Anne Cunningham

HIPPO HISTORY COLLAGE

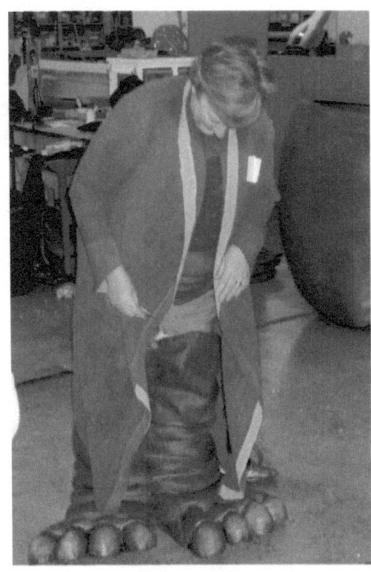

Creative technology

Prop

Somerset Festival of Literature

'Alyssa' painted by Margaret Storey—favourite book on table

Aileen Hall: Nanjing Cultural Ambassador

T.V. Studio   Dromkeen sculpture—
                           includes hippo

Humpty Doo: Northern Territory Literacy visit

Mobile library van

Darwin: Getting into books

CHAPTER 9
HIGHLIGHTS OF HIPPO HISTORY

100 Memories

Q. How can you have a history of a character who is imaginary?
A. It's based on facts of a kind. This is not a fake history.

First published in 1980, the original There's a Hippopotamus on Our Roof Eating Cake was conceived in 1978 after our new roof leaked. Deborah Niland's illustrations are now part of many children's imaginative history. The simplicity and reassurance of a big, colourful imaginary friend with all the answers, seems to reassure, especially children with special challenges.

The Hippocampus is the part of the brain where memory-forming, organising and imagination reside. Mine is almost full, especially after 40 years of creating stories, but the cake-eating hippo is the character for whom readers have the greatest affection and which attracts the quirkiest anecdotes.

The value for families in reading 'fantasy' is the encouragement of imaginative problem-solving and where it is OK to have 'fun' and to 'risk' trying a different way to solve a challenge. Quirky things happen to authors, or maybe they just note them. Apart from relieving boredom, it enriches life to have a sense of humour, which memorises the absurd, or juxta-poses unexpected combinations.

These 100 memories are random, and not ordered by significance nor date.

1. Knock at my front door. Small child. 'Excuse me. Is this the house where the hippo lives on the roof?' Answer: 'Have a look.'

2. Danish Palace note of thanks (with gold crown) from Princess Mary for autographed Hippo book Australia Government sent as official gift of the imagination for the birth of her daughter.

3. Fan letter addressed to: The Hippo, Blackburn South, and delivered in person to author by the smiling mailman.

4. Children love 'touching' the character. The power of fantasy is that children don't seem to have a problem with an imaginary friend taking on other forms, like an author prop of a stuffed toy, or being sculpted in metal. Former Literature Homestead Gallery Dromkeen sculpture of favourite book characters entwined, including cake-eating hippo, is now situated in front of Melbourne's State Library.

5. Youfu West Street Primary International School, Nanjing, China—2008. English teacher Shi Jing delivered an awe-inspiring English lesson to her Grade 4 Chinese students after she memorised the whole book *Look, There's a Hippopotamus in the Playground Eating Cake*.

    She prepared a powerpoint presentation of the scanned pages of the book (pictures and English text), timed to match her retelling of the story, during which she used relevant props.

    At the end, she asked the students questions and was thrilled that they had understood, even the concept of an imaginary friend. Fantasy crosses cultures.

6. Principal, an ex-rugby player, accepted challenge to eat cake on school roof, in hippo costume, and read the book aloud if his students surpassed their reading quotas. They did. And despite being scared of heights, he kept his promise.

7. 'That was my favourite book when I was a child,' Bearded bikie with tatts passing an autographing in a bookshop, while pre-schoolers listened wide-eyed. 'Reading's cool!'

8. Most 'nicked' library book. Compliment?

9. Father complained that he had to read that book every night to his children. Millions of times.

10. Hippopotamuseum created by gifted educator to demonstrate physics principles e.g. falling, related to Hippo character.

11. Mobile Library van which had hippo character painted outside and the books inside. Rural children chose popular book characters to be painted, and remain for ten years on the side of the mobile book van, which visits schools in the Shepparton region.

12. Rural prep mother who could not read, but wanted 'Another easy book like Hippo which I'm learning to read with my 5-year-old.' Brave woman to ask in front of other parents.

13. Creature Technology warehouse, with giant dinosaurs but also cake-eating film hippo puppet parts being made by brilliant craftspeople. A buzz of creativity. Magic moment.

14. Slices from numerous artistically Hippo-shaped cakes and easier flat 'roof cakes' plus a complaint that hippo was not eating gluten-free.

15. 'My Mum went to Weight Watchers, I think you should go too.' (fan e-mail to Hippo).

16. Edinburgh film festival entry tag. Left the 'e' off cake in the title … 'hippo eating cak' Scottish thrift or accent?

17. Estate agents' billboard voluntarily advertising a reading at the library with giant Hippo book cover slowed Werribee Freeway traffic!

18. Buying a two-seater Toyota Echo car, I asked, 'Will my hippo fit on the front passenger seat?' Answer: 'Of course Madam'.

19. Police breathalyser squad waving my car on with, 'Drive on Ma'am', after recognising my hippo passenger strapped in front seat.

20. Standing ovation at St Kilda Film Festival premiere after marshals kept the queues in line for the Pocket Bonfire film version of first Hippo screening.

21. Giant Book cover touring outback Northern Territory in back of a truck, and shown at libraries and festivals to encourage literacy. Within the book cover, a hole for child's head, so children became part of the book and were photographed as literacy incentive.

22. Parent's letter from children's hospital, thanking for the reassurance of *Hippo on the Hospital Roof* read in casualty waiting room and in ambulance en route.

23. In Nepali Montessori School, in Kathmandu reading through interpreter, with hippo music and dancing, and Himalayan mountains as a backdrop.

24. In Paris, at the now defunct Australian Bookshop, seeing Hippo displayed and talking with ex-pat families. Then reading at the American School with 25 nationalities in the room.

25. Hippo memorabilia collector from Peru, requested an autographed copy.

26. 'Hip Hip Hippo' on stage with 'Skylark Theatre' puppets and child from audience talking to the hippo puppet on roller-skates in the aisle, as if it were real.

27. Ushered to my mid-row author seat at the Canberra theatre premiere and very nervous about the first audience of adult sponsors, not children. Remembered seeing playwright Alan Seymour sitting alone in back row of a Melbourne Theatre premiere of one of his plays and slipping out mid-

way. I wanted to sit in the back seat, just in case. Hemmed in, I couldn't escape mid-performance and then first ripple of laughter from audience at the puppet production. It worked! Relief.

28. Braille hippo copy with 'feelie' illustrations shared with sighted children too. Braille bookmark in hippo shape.

29. Feelix suitcase of book and stimulus for blind pre-schoolers. Also had hippo cake tins, an audio and Braille copy. Helped name Feelix project. Felix means happy and 'feel' related to the textures felt by blind children.

30. Studio recording of extra (unpublished) hippo stories for use with disabled children and realizing they had a rhythm. Later these became the *Hand-Me-Down Hippo* female cousin chapter anthology illustrated by Mini Goss. 'Hand-Me-Down' was passing on something of value to a younger person.

31. Auslan signed video for deaf students: I can now 'sign' 'I love Hippo' and I shared a table with award-winning educators who silent 'clapped' in sign language. Fabulous teachers.

32. Nanjing School for the Blind swapping copies in different kinds of Braille.

33. Perth Airport photograph taken under Outsized Baggage with Hippo prop.

34. In Box Hill Hospital with 'Streptococcus Agalactica' and night nurses wanting books signed before I went to the ward.

35. Collage of memorable fan letters touring as 'Corridors of Characters' with Hippo responses by ghost-writer Hazel exhibited at the former Fremantle Maximum Security Jail.

36. Channel 31 *Kids in the Kitchen* television program with grandson cooking hippo-footprint pancakes on camera and making a joke about 'separating eggs' by putting them either end of the bench.
37. 'Hippo' PJs. Worn in Swanston Street, Melbourne Parade accompanying Dromkeen Literature Homestead float of children's ten favourite book characters.
38. Reading 'hippo' via torchlight in a dark nightclub film fun-raiser with aged twenty-something enthused fans.
39. 'The Two of Us' feature article about how the hippo perceives the author.
40. C.V. of a rooftop hippo requested, despite him being speechless, so author had to ghost-write previous jobs like roof-climbing and cake-testing.
41. Requested set of autographed hippo books as wedding gift.
42. Reading the story, via translator, in Auslan signing, Chinese and Braille sharing.
43. Fan mail peaks around Book Week and hippo gets his own e-mails. 'I haven't got a friends, will you come and sit on my roof' was the most poignant, which I answered in character.
44. 'Us mob like your stories. We laugh at the funny bits.' From an online webchat with a remote outback school.
45. 'Does the Hippo talk to Plato?' (*Plato the Platypus Plumber (Part-time)* is the John Petropoulos–illustrated picture book.) Imagine if one imaginary creature from one book could talk to another one? I answered, 'Yes, in my head.' Then I played with the idea of a party inviting them all. Catering could be a challenge, especially with a duck as the guest.

46. Being known or introduced as 'the Hippo lady' at my size and height is an ambiguous title.

47. Facebook thanks from mother of 13-year-old who'd had severe health challenges and who 'wore out' several hippo books by daily readings and these had been replaced regularly by the family.

48. Little 'pink' girl mouthing every word-for-word and dressed as the character.

49. 'Smack' support when furore about whether the word 'smack' should be replaced, in the new Penguin edition, with 'Daddy growled'.

50. At bookstore signing a girl called 'Angel' gave me a letter to give to the hippo 'who lives with you on your roof'.

51. 'This imaginary friend of yours is 35 years old ... and not married yet?' said a parent during a bookstore autographing session.

52. Retrieving the hippo from the baggage carousel at the airport, when surrounded by corporate types in suits with briefcases. Hippo just fitted in trolley.

53. Discovering that hippo can travel free as a 'tool of trade' in plane hold, rather than as excess baggage.

54. Putting hippo on wheels, like pull-along luggage, for fast travel but his bottom got dirty where he overlapped.

55. Bookstore kindly provided candles on the hippo cake. I blew them out quickly, just before the smoke detector above shrieked.

56. After a literary festival, the over-loved hippo needed cleaning. Dry cleaners wouldn't touch it because the head had paper inside. Too big to fit in washing machines, hippo had to be 'emptied' of the filling of polystyrene balls and the

'skin' washed by hand in baby soap flakes. Experts advised removing the filling either in the carpark or in the bath ... I found out why. The polystyrene balls went everywhere, even clung to our underwear. I hand washed 'skinny' hippo in our bath and a visitor freaked on opening the bathroom door to discover hippo hanging from the shower to dry.

57. An American request for an embroidery square of book character for a favourite author quilt. Flattering, but I'm hopeless at sewing. My neighbour came to the rescue and did a hippo square within the 48-hour limit. The school had sent American stamps for a reply-paid envelope, not realising Australians have their own stamps.

58. Hippo-collectors exist. They buy anything to do with hippos. Others collect frogs or cats.

59. Face-lift. A friend mended the hippo when his seams split and the original 'pattern' couldn't be traced. The 'face-lift' altered his expression and his eyebrows became menacing rather than kindly. Quick nips and tucks were necessary. (Downsizing to a bee, next.)

60. Being asked to autograph a 'pre-loved' copy, with cover damaged by over-use, and embarrassed parent. Author response: 'Great to see a book being so well read.'

61. Ladder-Climbing Competency. Due to Education departmental rules, no staff allowed to climb above their own height without a ladder climbing competency certificate. We forged one for hippo so the local newspaper reporter could capture the hippo climbing the ladder onto the mobile library van roof.

62. Hand-Me-Down. A Queensland special school student designed a patchwork Hand-Me-Down Hippo by sticking on bits and I thought it was a brilliant idea. A patchwork made from bits of other treasures. The Hand-Me-Down Hippo

has been passed onto the next generation as the treasured idea of friendship and reassurance.

63. I.D. During a family crisis, I was dropped at Tullamarine Airport by my daughter who accidently took my handbag containing my ticket, credit cards and I.D. Helpful airstaff accepted my author photo on the back of my book as I.D., re-issued a ticket and sent my handbag on the next flight to Launceston. A Good Samaritan in the queue gave me a few dollars for a coffee. 'You'll need this.' When interviewed on radio as part of an author tour, the next day, I made a public thank you and swore I'd keep my P.R. photo on books up to date.

64. Naming characters and titles is a challenge. I used to pay my son $1 per title, until he left home. Apt titles matter and each hippo book in the series must start with different words for easy cataloguing. Thirty-nine rejected titles is my record. Asked for suggestions and was swamped.

65. Fantasy logic dilemma of former unisex baby in earlier hippo books, now older and needs a pronoun. Readers got mixed up and wanted to name Hippo too. 'Amus' meaning friend was the suggested name, taken from hippopotamus.

66. Question Mark candles. Now fashionable, not just for hippo cakes, to match any aged reader but to re-use for people who prefer to be vague about their age. I didn't want a specific number of candles on any cake illustration, so the hippo was age-less or the age of the reader.

67. Classroom performances of the playscripts inspired by the picture books have included 'dual language' acting, with students speaking their own first language. Hippo doesn't speak so pillow stuffed hippos were popular actors.

68. Car passenger. Friend suggested I could legitimately travel in the freeway fast lane to the airport, as the front seat-belt-

ed hippo qualified as a passenger.

69. During a heavy storm, Prep children told the librarian it must be the hippo on their school roof.

70. Despite having own original set, Grandson borrowed and lost hippo book from school library. Asked to replace it, and replied 'My Grandma wrote that.'

71. School librarians greeted me in their hippo PJs during an author visit. And for a casual dress literary day, their secondary school girls bought every pair available locally, some even sharing tops or bottoms.

72. Zoo launch near hippo enclosure. Guests invited to BYOHF (Bring Your Own Hippo Food) e.g. hippo dandruff white marshmallows & hippo blood red wine for adults and cordial for children.

73. Feelix Pre-Schoolers project 2003 with 'graduates' in 2013 who could read and were articulate public speakers. Book investment paid off.

74. In top 20 favourite children's books of the century and Books a Child Should Own.

75. Auslan signed editions made by the College of the Deaf for hearing-impaired children in 2003.

76. My grandson visited Japan on school tour. The hippo book was published and translated in Japanese a generation before he was born!

77. Americans don't have caravans and wanted to change the wording to mobile home, or make the food healthier and delete the cake.

78. 'It was my favourite book when I was a child.' Thirty-ish boyfriend bought signed copy for girlfriend for Christmas.

79. Pocket Bonfire film-makers Jaime & Joel were hippo fans when children. Being child-readers was an imaginative investment. Then they created the film of the hippo.
80. Standing ovation at St Kilda Film festival for hippo film.
81. Many dads and Beaut Blokes do great funny voices reading.
82. *Hand-Me-Down Hippo* chapter stories are of a female cousin hippo, illustrated by Mini Goss. 'Handed down' to a new generation like a favourite toy to someone younger or smaller.
83. Real hippos eat carrots. Maybe carrot cake too?
84. Fan made a hippo finger puppet. Neighbour gave me a hippo bath plug and toothbrush.
85. I'm a minimalist, not a collector, but a producer from TV *Collectors* program looked at the hippo memorabilia I'd been given and decided it was insufficient for a program. Russian Fabergé egg with a hippo on roof inside was made by a family friend. Hippo stamps are useful for autographing but hippo soap and toothbrush holder I could live without.
86. Radio Talkback. 'Why doesn't the hippo answer instead of you?'
87. Many hand-made books, usually by Prep children, modelled on Hippo story shape.
88. The baby's name is Just Right. Young reader's solution to un-named baby.
89. Why are there three clicks of the seat-belt and four people in the car? Simultaneous clicking?
90. I know where Hippo lives, 'Half past Grandma.' Probably because Grandma is a location and time is measured in

half hours.

91. At Christmas, Santa Claus must use skylights for his reindeers because no chimneys in our place. Will he see hippo there on the roof? The challenge of fictional characters co-existing.

92. At the Islamic school, they offered Turkish delight instead of cake for the visiting hippo.

93. Literary Lunch: Individual cupcakes, with gluten-free or other appropriate food for children with allergies.

94. Listed on all-time favourite children's picture book collection, international touring exhibition.

95. Donated original stuffed hippo to Canberra University's Lu Rees Collection of Children's Literature and Japanese visitors love it.

96. The new model 2 Hippo originally sat on a model roof and had a broom stick inside to keep vertical. But roof was damaged during a festival and 'floppy' hippo, minus broomstick, stayed in my backroom with occasional visits to schools.

97. 'Borrowed' hippo was returned sitting in the back of a truck, with the courier's notebook listing it as: 'Animal delivery'.

98. Hippo's library bag was useful for carrying Braille copy and had H on the bag for Hippo. But his cake often fell off. Eventually it was sewn on.

99. Librarian provided a band-aid for Hippo for the hospital story.

And 100. Asked if Cake-Eating Hippo has his own #hashtag? That hasn't happened yet.

Occasionally I have a qualm. I love all my book children. Will my other 'characters' get upset at constant Hippo attention? Crafting problem-solvers like Quintana who figures things out in *The Hundreds and Thousands Kid* has given me more personal satisfaction. But Hippo gets all the attention.

Q. How Did You Feel About a Film or Theatre Being Made from Your Picture Book?

Short answer: Thrilled that my story has gone into another creative dimension.

Longer Answer: A book is a bit like a child. At some stage you have to let it go out on its own.

For me, the greatest creative satisfaction is the moment of capturing the abstract idea in words, before it goes onto the page or screen. The second is when a reader takes those word clues and uses their own imagination to re-create an approximation of the idea I was playing with. Then it becomes their story, not mine.

The third is when a 'fan' contacts me to share that something special has happened as a result of my book.

And that's what happened with the making of the film. Pocket Bonfire film-makers Jaime Snyder and Joel Sharpe contacted me, as a result of reading the favourite book as children, and inspired to make a film. To me that was the greatest compliment, to offer to take my book-baby into a medium in which they are skilled.

To be invited to the workshop of Creatures Technology to see the hippo which had been created by their people as in-kind support for the project was thrilling. A massive warehouse, with gigantic models of dinosaur creatures, roof-high, and a buzz of creative enjoyment in the quality of the problem they were solving in hippo parts design. I tried on the feet and needed help to get out of them. I marvelled at the mouth. And the hippo backside. And felt the skin texture. But I also felt the communal creativity of imaginative problem solving, in another dimension.

Seeing the completed film was poignant for me. It was as if I were outside myself, watching how an author is supposed to react to their film. I think Pocket Bonfire were concerned that I would be pedantic about keeping to the book, but I was intrigued by how they had developed the story, keeping to the essence of the original. The girl is older and there's implied tension between parents but the need for an imaginary friend is still there. At first I felt the hippo was a little scary, but later versions were emotionally and symbolically more balanced.

My daughter Kim came with me to the mainly twenty-something crew-cast screening, and the ownership and pride of the participants at all levels was a thrilling experience. Much in-kind support, even to the neighbour's ladder up to the roof for the hippo on the film set. 'Did you see that ladder?' I was asked at the showing. 'That's mine! Great film.'

Thank you Jaime and Joel for giving me and the audience the gift of imagination and taking my book into the film world.

CHAPTER 10
CHOOSING APT TITLES

Kids' Questions

Surreal sayings by kids make great titles.

After again keying in 'There's a Hippopotamus on Our/My Roof Eating Cake', the appeal of one-word, short titles is apparent. Embarrassed to say that after umpteen years, I still have to check whether it is 'my', 'the' or 'our' roof because one edition inadvertently used the wrong pronoun, and I can never remember which.

Now there are other equally challenging titles in the series, because to prevent cataloguing librarians going into a decline, each title must start with a different word. And yet the series need to be instantly recognisable.

Thirty-nine temporary titles or work in progress (W.I.P.) titles is my upper record. Often marketing departments decree the final title. Meta-tags have increased in importance, but it's easy to miscue a fantasy in the wrong categories. Hippo—Cake—Rooftop can mean going into the foody area of master chef, architecture or wildlife listings.

My *Between Us*, an early drama education title, was mis-filed in the health area as a sex manual. Whereas an earlier version of *Friends* was called *Friends Love Sex* with no punctuation and sold very well. Later the e-version was renamed *Friends: How to Make and Keep Them*. Mundane but functional.

Book titles can last even longer than the child you name, who may not go out of print but change, by deed poll or nickname, the wonderful name you chose for them. So authors have a responsibility to choose wisely.

Feymouse, an ambiguous title for a picture book app, depends very much on the speaker's accent. Said quickly, it becomes 'Famous' which was one intention, since it's a satire of 'the myth of celebrity', a large and clumsy cat 'Fey' born into a family of highly talented mice. Inspired by young fan who wanted to be a 'feymouse arthur' when she grew up. Lots of kids want to be arthurs (authors).

A character name as the title isn't enough to entice a reader, unless they share the name. Parents will always buy a picture book where their child's name is the major character, whether they are rabbits, dinosaurs or bears. 'Ruby', 'Oliver' and 'Ethan' are currently popular.

Autographing children's books gives authors and illustrators the 'hot goss' on popular names. Geographic locations (where the child was conceived or the parents thought about having a baby) are in fashion.

Dakota, Paris, London, Savannah, Sahara, Atlanta, Siena, Rome, Sydney, Phoenix, Boston, Malaya and Darwin are currently real children for whom I've signed books. Siblings include India, China and more recently Asia and Antarctica.

Climate Change parents have chosen Summer, Winter, Skye, Storm and names of various winds like Sirocco or Mistral. No Thunder or Lightning yet.

Sub-Titles

Non fiction often has a sub title. I wanted to use *Hi-Healers* for a commissioned series of interviews with high profile women about serious health issues and their coping strategies. But the publisher decreed *Healthy Women: Getting the Balance Right* could be found more easily in a database.

'Write your own story, just using the titles of your favourite author.'

An imaginative educator set students the task of each writing an original story using all the titles of their chosen author. Only 'and' or 'but' were allowable extras. Despite the maths, some didn't choose the one-book-title author. It's a great compliment to have students create a story from your 200 titles. Also ensures you use shorter titles in future.

A memorable title for an autobiography or a history is hard. Usually I avoid phrases because people forget them. A key word like 'Non-Boring' and unexpected juxtaposing of ideas helps. Three words where the last is unexpected like 'Did, Done, Dead' (which I'm saving for a family history). I liked the conciseness of 'Betwixt' for a short story I wrote on an intergender child.

f2m: the boy within was a very careful title, conceived during the Cappuccino Approach with illustrator Felicity Marshall in a café where we brainstormed ideas for titles, scribbling them on paper placemats (and keying into my digital device).

Dating

E-mail Murder Mystery was a technology-based mystery which dated rapidly and the clues were no longer relevant for new readers, so best not to use a technical term in the title. My mistake. Today it would be easy to track a suspect via digital clues which didn't exist then.

Snail Mail also dated and became a common term for non digital mail. Originally my picture book title was *Snail Mail Trail* but that's a bit hard to say after a few drinks.

Political Correctness

Western Australia suffered from rabbit plagues and the Mallee had mice. I never used 'Rabbits' in my titles but I had the odd mouse.

Mystery series titles like *The Frequent Flyer Twins* included *The Idea Pirates* which changed relevance as more people began to speak about pirating intellectual property.

Strictly speaking, the title *Stalker* should be *Stalkee*, because the main character Lily is stalked, but that sounds like a flower or plant.

'Tag' the short story was about colloquial use of that term by graffiti artists as well as being the shortest title I've ever used and for which I am grateful when filling in forms.

Discussing Literature became affectionately known by students as 'Disgusting Literature'. *Birds on the Brain* was about the birds released at weddings. Replaced the working title of 'Birdbrain' which had negative connotations of being stupid.

The challenge for an author is that you may have several groups of readers who use the title words in different ways. Or language usage changes. Frankly, it's a bit like kids and nicknames.

CHAPTER 11
COME AND MEET MY CAMEL

Invitation I Couldn't Refuse

'Come and meet my camel.'

How could I refuse? Especially as the dad was an adventurous Indiana Jones look-alike in khaki shorts, wide brimmed hat and boots. Plus the three racing camels. One for the 10-year-old, another for his dad and the third camel for the visiting author.

The 'camel offer' came while speaking to children and adult groups at the mining settlement of Mt Newman, having flown in from Port Hedland, across a red desert with a snaking train line below. Even over Paraburdoo ... ('It's 42 at Paraburdoo' was the frequent ABC radio weather forecast). I was thrilled to discover Paraburdoo is a real place, not just a rhyming weather and temperature forecast. BHP Billiton is an Anglo-Australian multinational mining, metals and petroleum company and they were sponsoring me 'as culture' and put me up at the S.P.Q. (Single Persons' Quarters) rambling but comfortable accommodation units with beds, showers and a mess–dining room for meals. (And a mysterious lacy bra hanging in the ladies' showers from a bike handbar. Will reveal all later.)

Mt Newman is 1,186km north of Perth in the heart of the East Pilbara, one of the most isolated regions, where summer temperatures hover over 40°C and weather changes without warning. So when I'm asked about the more extreme places I've visited: Mt Newman, Antarctica, Kathmandu in Nepal and Balikpapan—in Indonesia's East Kalimantan, with the orphaned Orangutans and gated, guarded international community—get a mention.

A new language to learn. S.P.Q. is Single Persons' Quarters, the local mine workers accommodation. F.I.F.O.s are Fly In, Fly Out workers whose families often live elsewhere, but Mt Newman has a large proportion of residential families with young children, hence my invitation. Plus an enterprising librarian who had painted foot and paw prints leading into her library to entice young non-readers to visit. It worked.

After we'd had a class chat that morning on 'senses' writing including the smells, sounds, sight and habits of imaginary and real pets, the 10-year-old thought I'd like to desert road–test the camel after school. He and his mine-worker dad belonged to the Newman Camel Riders' Club. Their aim was to ride to Uluru next school holidays and take part in the annual camel race.

'Use my Sharna in your next story,' he suggested.

Instead of the usual cats, dogs and cake-eating hippos, is what he meant.

'I feed her, but she's young and not completely trained yet.'

That swaying 'ship of the desert' called Sharna may make it into a story one day. Camel-habits included. And my sore backside was fun research on the other camel too.

What Happens on a National Book Tour?

At Melbourne's Tullamarine Airport, the baggage attendant looked warily at my cardboard-boxed big book of *There's a Hippopotamus on My Roof Eating Cake*.

'Better take it with you luv, they're the sort of things that get lost.'

I had no intention of losing my 'prop', which was essential for two planned Hippo parties and any large-scale young audiences who needed to see 'from the back'.

Digital developments have made carrying props easier ... USBs of electronic jewellery are lighter than 'real' books. However, the baggage system was excellent, even a fan photo taken of me and the hippo under Outsized Baggage at the airport.

Officials often have kids or grandkids and 'Hippo' opens bureaucratic doors. And the baggage-handlers did not lose copies of my picture book *Not Lost, Just Somewhere Else*. Maybe the title did have something to do with that.

Looking at my eight-day itinerary, I wondered: would my voice last the distance? Nine sessions on the second day! Diplomatically, the organiser suggested to local librarians that the load be reduced.

Ex-Melbourne on a 9 a.m. flight, I arrived at Port Hedland 4.30 p.m. local time. I began to realise the distances involved and how planes are used like buses by locals. A zany ex-model with a wonderful sense of humour, the librarian wore massive ear-rings and her staff took on the role of author-minders with great efficiency. A quick conducted tour of Hedland pointing out the two towns, South and Port, and indicating the schools I would visit.

At Cemetery Beach, turtles bobbed and intriguing historical gravestones of the Asian cooks, divers and fishermen were found in the Pioneers' Cemetery. Hedland did have potential story material and that's what I tried to suggest in all sessions. It's worth writing about your own area.

Sunday morning at the Cooke Point school fete to read stories and judge the colouring competition, a new experience because I prefer students to draw their own rather than keep inside the lines. An ex–naval commander turned artist was my fellow judge. I left the artistic decisions to him and offered to write up the comments and announce the winners on the microphone. In the Year 7 category I announced a singular prize. There was only one entry.

Often visiting authors are invited to judge Literary Lunches, where students have made food to link to book titles. If pressed, I always avoid the elaborately iced entries by parents who did the cake-decorating courses and choose 'The Most Imaginative' or 'The Most Improved', as an encouragement. Best was the rub-on stick of Mum deodorant with Wagon Wheel chocolate biscuits stuck either side for my *Mum on Wheels* book.

Literary Tourism can be generated because an award winning book was set in that location or inspired by a former resident. The Alan Marshall association with Noorat in Victoria, pronounced 'N'rat', not 'New rat', started an *I Can Jump Puddles* festival. Often I suggest locals research their literacy legacies via 'genis', the colloquial name for family historians.

Cake shops get a boost from author visits. South Hedland Library's 'Hippo Party' provided a magnificent hippo-shaped cake as well as games and stories organised for about thirty pre-schoolers and parents. Photographs were taken, with parental permission, for the local paper, and I provided a caption mentioning the tour sponsor, as it's vital to support those prepared to sponsor book tours. With the increase in food allergies amongst children, providing cakes for book launches can be challenging. I was asked why my hippo character hadn't specified that his cake was gluten free. It wasn't. Then the dairy intolerant group requested a special cake too. Solution is to provide cup cakes for individuals so no children miss out on literary treats.

Monday was the heavy day. Anticipating this and with a body still two hours out on Melbourne time, I swam at 6 a.m. Schools start early because of the heat, and by 8.30 a.m. my minder had deposited me at St Cecilia's to meet the welcoming library teacher. Year 6/7 had an hour's session followed by Year 3/4 and then the Preps, plus Years 1 and 2. Quickly I autographed the existing school copies of my books. A new minder appeared to transport me to Cooke Point for the unexpected extra session: 11.45 a.m.—12.15 p.m. with Grade 6 in the library. Five sessions before lunch! The children were pleasant but with similarly aged groups, it's difficult to remember to whom I said what. I know there are some authors and illustrators who have a set script, but I always improvise. But I did remember the child who asked 'Are you a witch, Hazel?'

A quick salad in the staffroom where new teachers compared bus timetables on how long it would take to travel back to Perth on the first day of the next holidays. On the staffroom table was my unopened magazine interview with Dr Ergad Gold on how to encourage creative problem-solving in children. Meanwhile the teachers decided that the Pioneer bus service was faster because it didn't do the milk run, backtracking into small towns.

I was scheduled to be in the library at 12.20 p.m. to meet interested children who wanted stories, followed by a class of Year 7s from 12.45 p.m.—1.30 p.m. I took my coffee with me. My throat needed lubrication.

On to South Hedland Primary—set in tropical lushness and with a welcoming sign in English, Indonesian, Arabic and several local Aboriginal languages. This Year 5 class asked some of the most thoughtful and interesting questions and had obviously been well prepared. Sessions like this are not a strain on the author, who can answer genuinely rather than feel obliged to 'perform'.

'What kind of suggestions do you make to the illustrator?'

'Do you think of the idea first, or decide on the shape, whether it will be book or play or cartoon?'

'If you like the character will you give him an extra story in another book?'

Early afternoon, we arrived at the red earth playground of Cassia Primary, which sensibly shared facilities with the Education Centre. Students had rehearsed 'Helmetella', a safety satire of Cinderella, but on bikes, from my *Playsafe* collection which they performed as part of the book launch. The script was acted with great gusto, with many legal bike laps and a few illegal 'show offs', then a question and answering session with me, as the author, for about 20 minutes.

Launches work best at school where the theme of the book is turned into a fun activity which has photographic possibilities for the local newspaper or TV. These bikes and riders looked colourful in action shots. And because the Child Accident Prevention organisation had sponsored the original play collection, there was media interest in the health and safety issue.

Parents, teachers, librarians and students made up the audience of about 80. Next book launch there'll be no shortage of actors. And scripts are easy reading with a purpose. Action Literacy means you read while doing. Just pack a First Aid kit.

Back to the hotel for the 'Meet the Author' dinner with local librarians, teachers and interested writers. The St Cecilia librarian read out some 'unedited' letters to the author written by her children as a result of the morning visit.

Us Mob Like Your Stories

'Us mob like your stories too.'

Such a genuine compliment. 'Us mob' is used widely in fan mail from indigenous kids.

Melbourne children from Blackburn Lake Primary had sent questions for me to ask children on remote stations.

- Do you have pets or are they all working animals?
- If your mum is your teacher, what happens when you don't do your homework?
- Who do you play with?
- What if all the children want to talk at the same time, on the air?
- Would you like to swap with our school for a week?

I left the questions to be given to the School of the Air teacher who had radio links to students in far flung cattle stations.

On to beautiful Broome with its well-known resort Cable Beach, and local initiatives such as Magabala Books. *Magabala* is the word used in many Aboriginal languages of the Kimberley for the bush banana which, when dry, disperses seeds that travel a long way in the wind. Apt symbolism.

At the Aboriginal-controlled publishing house, we shared the challenges of storytelling, researching, writing and illustrating books. Some subjects of indigenous culture are sacred and cannot be published. Others have to be checked by elders which lengthens the editorial process, considerably. In addition, Magabala Books have the extra design challenge of setting dual-language books where words take up double space on the page. I'm interested in this design challenge for other dual-language books too. And for those who have a mainly oral storytelling culture. Technology is offering new ways of sharing stories, but the culture has to be respected.

'Broome time is different,' explained Stefan, the Town Librarian who didn't wear a watch. Many claim he has the best job in Australia for the flexibility of hours and attitudes. A quick drive around the town culminated in two mango–lemon–lime drinks at Cable Beach, Lord Alpine's resort establishment, before tackling, at Broome pace, the author schedule.

The evening session was at Broome Library, a cool, shuttered, tropical building with lazy fans (of the ceiling variety) reminiscent of novel settings by Graham Greene or Somerset Maugham. The dozen enthusiastic participants included two part-time freelance journalists writing for local newspapers, who took photographs to accompany their stories. One was watchless, but had a broken clock in her handbag. Evidence that Broome is another time dimension.

For the locals, it was winter, so they wore jumpers, but I was beginning to feel the heat. At 8.30 a.m. at the High school, the teacher offered to turn on the air conditioning for me. How do they cope with 48 degrees in the summer? The most frequent questions was, 'How much money do authors make?'

In country areas, radio staff are multi-talented, conducting interviews as well as panel-operating, talkback and music. Often the staff is one person. She conducted the ABC radio interview, glancing at author bio notes and asking penetrating questions as well as handling the microphone levels. Next door, the owner of the Kimberley Bookshop, the only bookshop in the entire region, vanished into the studio to do her book reviews on air, so we adjourned for a freshly squeezed apple-and-lemon drink at the Baghdad Café. From the verandah, we watched the backpackers, pearl buyers and tourists. Returning to the studio we chatted about book distribution and the problems of booksellers. Local histories and glossy photographic books are popular, but 'Teachers don't buy many books. Not many of them read for pleasure,' explained the bookseller.

Magabala Books are prominently displayed and sell well, but few children's books were available.

'We had a few of yours, but they sold,' said the bookshop owner. Was that a compliment?

Broome Primary was a tropical delight with damp gardens, shady verandahs and eager children. One Prep child kept fiddling with my leg as I read them a story. Only later I realised I was wearing black panty hose and most women have bare legs in Broome. Why did I have black-skinned legs but white arms and face?

Broome time was affecting me. Knowing Librarian Stefan didn't have a watch, I hurried to finish the second session by 2 p.m. so I wouldn't miss the 2.30 p.m. plane.

'I thought you'd had enough and that's why you were finishing early,' grinned Stefan as he unlocked the van door for me. 'Your plane doesn't go until 2.55.' We went and had another lemon–lime and apple drink. Plane was delayed anyway.

During the flight to Hedland, the weather deteriorated. At Paraburdoo, the plane couldn't land and went onto Newman airfield which was wet, windswept and surrounded by red mud.

'In the olden days they used to ferry passengers to the airfield in the shovel end of a front—loader,' explained the librarian expertly handling her four wheel drive vehicle.

'BHP has arranged for you to stay at the SPQ in J47.'

Translated. The mining company offered free accommodation and meals in their Single Persons Quarters. Next morning, I hesitantly entered the Mess three blocks down, but the 6 a.m. shift had already gone. Generous mess helpings of porridge, mushrooms, spaghetti, eggs and toast, with unlimited self serve toast, coffee, milk and juice. Apart from the attendant, I was the only woman amongst the tattooed, muscled workers. Navy singlets are the only fashion. Talking doesn't require as much food-fuel as driving a Haulpak, blasting ridges or fixing massive machinery, so I stuck to muesli and coffee.

Unfamiliar with mining, the sheer size of the iron-ore mine and even the wheels on the Haulpak were illuminating. When children later suggested 'A Hippo working on a Haulpack', I could relate to local conditions.

Library storytelling with double groups of toddlers and parents was noisily successful and books were autographed. How many thousand times had I said the word 'Hippo'? At least I had other titles. A one-book author would be in a word warp. Later, a minder warned me confidentially that after a week of escorting a well-known author, she could do the word-for-word-talk-script herself.

Questions flowed from well-prepared Year 6/7 South Newman students. In the afternoon, two sessions at Newman Primary were supervised by relief teachers. This meant opportunities for follow-ups were lost. The Hippo Tea was for about 30 invited children and held inside due to the weather. More picture-poster judging and book prizes to autograph.

The evening 'creative writing' workshop attracted only three adults including the President of the local Fellowship of Australian Writers, but a worthwhile session.

The Killer Question

Friday morning was a solid three hours at the high school. Writing anecdotes won over the Year 9s, but older students wanted to know about teenagers elsewhere.

'Ok, that's your literary research. Interview me,' I offered.

'But you're not 15.'

'True. But ... Try How, Where, When and Why Questions.

They work for all subjects when a writer may be trying to find out about an unknown. Or an interviewee may know things they didn't realise they knew.'

The class interest level soared.

'Want to know the Killer Question?' I asked.

Of course they did.

'What's the question you would least like me to ask you, and what is your answer?'

In return, I learnt about adolescent life in Newman, BBQs, roller discos, riding and racing, at the same time as suggesting what rich writing material they possessed. Teachers asked about writing techniques for animation and puppetry scripting, and it was helpful to share genuine examples of what could and had gone wrong.

'I didn't know puppeteers had to do warm-up leg exercises to strengthen their thighs to hold the puppets.'

'Next time I look at a minute of cartoons, I'll think about the weeks behind it.'

'Could we do a script about Haulpak at a mine?'

'Why not? Great red dirt setting.'

Two pleasant sessions at the kindergarten were followed by an open house at the library, where pre-loved books could be signed or people chat to the author. To save my voice, I listened, a lot. Then came the unexpected highlight, the camels.

Such thoughtfulness by the librarian in chasing up a camel-rider after the chance question to the 10-year-old about a pet camel. Worth scraping the mud off my only pair of shoes!

An informal dinner with library staff and partners, the presentation of a local watercolour, and a final night in the SPQ. At last! I met the mysterious female who left her bike, bra and brown work boots in the ladies' shower. She was a Maori mechanic, working shifts at the mine. Impressive lady.

On the Newman–Karratha flight, fellow-passenger singer Normie Rowe confided his desire to write a book. As a professional entertainer, he gets a buzz from performance. I was beginning to flag.

At the next stop of Karratha, the Cossack Fair was the weekend attraction. After a beautiful fish lunch, thoughtfully chosen because my bio-note said I liked fish, we drove to the historic Cossack, where storytelling was a BIG challenge.

The session was scheduled on the verandah of the Courthouse building between the popular Gents' Loo and the loud Bushband. We took photos to prove that we had transformed the corner-of-nothing verandah into an attractive storytelling area with 30–40 children passing through. After three sessions, when the band's noise level increased, I called it quits. Karratha librarians agreed we'd done a reasonable job.

No Voice Left

Sunday morning, two minutes before the plane left, a photo-journalist arrived with extra questions.

'How many children have you spoken to this week? Ten, a couple of hundred or a few thousand?'

Up until then I hadn't been counting.

'Probably close to the two thousand.'

'What were the most frequently asked questions?'

No 1. Where do you get your ideas from?

No 2. How many books have you written?

No 3. How much money do you make?

Against the mine wages, authors' incomes are minuscule. How do others judge the success of an author tour? Publicity for books and writing? Numbers of people involved? Support for those who provide ideas in remote regions? Literacy? Author exhaustion?

'Did you have a nice holiday?' asked my neighbour.

I nodded. No voice left.

CHAPTER 12
IS WRITING YOUR FAMILY TRADE?

Family Involvement:
Reluctant, Conscripted or Volunteered?

'Is writing your family trade?' was a recent question at a literary festival. I hadn't thought of authorship that way before, but probably the answer is 'yes'. My family has done the 'word' apprenticeship voluntarily, reluctantly or been conscripted.

The family of a writer can't help involvement in books, either reading them, inspiring or being captured as characters or caricatures in them. Even the dog or bird may get a role. Pets real or imaginary do feature. Bonuses include interesting dinner visitors, autographed copies by other authors and behind-the-scenes in TV studios, ship engine rooms, outback bush camps or researching in gliders or small planes. And then there are the tours; festivals or family visits to international Booktowns like Australia's Clunes. Even our 14-year-old grandson thought that a country town full of second-hand books was a 'cool' place to visit for a three-generational family weekend.

Family has to 'carry' the bag of books on wheels, answer a phone politely and host strangers with different food or cultural customs. They become travellers, not tourists.

Whether family becomes the 'raw material' is an ethical issue, as well as one of time-management.

Literary Terrorism

A frequent author question is: 'Do you put your family in your books?'

'No, that's literary terrorism, just putting the author's version or interpretation of relationships.'

But I have used family holiday settings, including French canal barges or Asian street markets, as background for fact or fiction. Or activities like playing hockey, soccer or orienteering have been given as hobbies to characters or provided authentic clues.

Living with the child or adolescent age group for whom you are writing is instant and unavoidable research into current trends. So is exposure to the latest technology and sports rules.

Having a mother or grandparent who writes professionally means a bit of ghost-writing occurs. But no pinching of ideas.

I remember my then eight-year-old grandson writing a terrific story from the viewpoint of A. Virus. The spelling needed a bit of work, but the concept was original. Much better than I could do. I resisted 'pinching' that idea, despite mentioning it now as a relevant example.

Garnet & Hazel Edwards

Family anecdotes are used. All families have funny stories of when things went wrong. Authors' tales are a little more public and around for longer. An incident involving a four-year-old may be captured in a book and that's available when he's a man. By the time he's parent-age, that's fine, but adolescents are always embarrassed by their family whether in print, in person or on screen.

Basically, something has to go wrong for a story to have dramatic interest. So authors tend to exaggerate 'real' mishaps and that's embarrassing. Like getting on the wrong bus in the USA and ending up in Plymouth, Massachusetts instead of Plymouth, New Hampshire. But much depends upon the tone of the 'telling' and whether it is laughing 'with' or 'at'. Self deprecation is better.

The age of the family matters. At certain stages, they are 'proud' of a book by Mum. In teen years they are embarrassed by anything public.

As children, my offspring used to give my stories the 'yawn test' and turn face down on the page which became boring. Ruthless. Candid. Effective. I always re-wrote after failing the yawn test—or at least scrapped the first chapter which was only introducing, and began at the dramatic bit.

Timely

Did you write for children because it was easier?

No. It was harder, but shorter.

Did I write for children because I had them as captive readers within the family?

Partly, it was a time-management decision.

Living with the appropriately-aged children meant instant research of legs in plaster, forgetful Tooth Fairies with the wrong change/overpayment in $10 notes, or current language updates such as 'sick' meaning the opposite.

Writing adult satire and writing for children is similar in process. Both are deceptively simple, and short, but there's subtext of more complex ideas beneath, and word placement is vital. So you can plot in your head, while changing nappies or cooking spaghetti (not simultaneously), and then write the ideas paragraphs which physically take little time to key. Each turns on unexpected viewpoint, like the view of the flea on the sea dog on the Titanic. Or thinking through the logic of what a rooftop, cake-eating hippo might do which is consistent with the fantasy.

So while young family life was most demanding, I wrote 'short' in snatched quarter-hours in the car during family pick-ups. With the first couple of books, my husband was an excellent proof-reader because, as a slow and thoughtful reader, he checked efficiently. I skim-read and see what I expect to be there, not what is, so I am a bad proof-reader. And I also prefer to move onto the next project. But after a couple of books, the novelty wore off, and he left proof-reading to me. Except for the time I was beset in the Antarctic polar ice and he proof-read the current project, as it looked like I might be in Antarctica for the whole year.

My generation of females has lived through interesting times sociologically. Reading biographies of women has sustained me through difficult times. In one sense I've traded my experiences with the reader. Participant-observation is a technique I've used. In *Trail Magic*, my son did all the walking and in *Cycling Solo: Ireland to Istanbul*, he did all the cycling. My daughter Kim is my marketing manager. A collaboration from which I've learnt to enter the digital world. Since he retired, my husband has done my accounts so I'm very grateful for that. 'His weekly miracle' he calls it as he juggles my 'other books'. The family trade continues.

Clunes Booktown Storytellers' Chair, with designer Clayton Edwards

CHAPTER 13
FAMILY & FRIENDS

Ideas on Legs

Dog-walking ideas can travel. My neighbour Cheryl has been my 'first' reader in suburbia, co–dog-walker (when we had dogs) and pram-pusher with toddlers ... someone unrelated to the literary world who gives valuable feedback on stories and listens to my frustrations! Her daughter Lani was the third child involved in our Hippo-book–writing after the dripping roof incident.

Cheryl read the draft *f2m: the boy within* to test mainstream reactions to the gender transition issues and later she met my co-author Ryan. She's been through the conception, pregnancy and birthing of many of my book babies. And the death of a few too ... (I won't add 'midwife' here. Maybe taking that analogy too far, but many writers compare the creativity of giving birth to books with giving birth to babies.)

Embarrassing moments have also been shared. Standing at the curb, waiting to cross the road with a toddler and two dogs, Cheryl said 'Sit!' and the toddler sat!

Or the time our Obedience School drop-out, in the dog-free park, lifted his leg on two amorous lovers in the grass. (Yes, I know it's the owners who fail at Obedience School, not the dogs.) As my husband dragged Phantom away, apologising, Cheryl and I dissolved in laughter, pretending we didn't know them.

'Phantom' was the inspiration for Tiny, the big dog in the *Project Spy Kids* series. Yes, the real Phantom did get a bucket of water over him for barking incessantly, and then I discovered he was warning us about the back fence on fire. Cheryl and I shared that too.

Having someone prepared to give a general readers' view on ideas has been invaluable. Wonderful friend and now I've alienated all the others whom I've not mentioned.

Parental Influences.

As an only child I had more time to explore other worlds via books. My theory is: if you are in a family of uneven numbers, you are forced to acquire the skills to make friends. If you are close to a sibling, there's always someone else around with whom to play. If not, you're forced to explore outside and observe how others relate. Books were idea-friends and gave insight into relationships, but I had 'real' people too. As a teenager I had a number of boyfriends, because not having brothers, I wanted to understand how male minds differed from female. Still trying to work that out.

I never saw being an only child as a liability, just the norm for me. And my friends were chosen on enthusiasms, not age.

Mum loved exaggerating potential disasters. If the sun was shining, there was a storm just ahead, but she was brilliant at collecting friends. Her neighbours and friends were usually dependents with problems which made her feel needed and allowed to be bossy about minor details. Hope the bossy bit isn't genetic, but the capacity to make friends is a skill passed onto my children and for which I'm grateful.

Highly anxious, my mother was apprehensive about any new venture. Adventure and risk were not in her vocabulary. Getting married to my father in her early thirties was risky. An agnostic, he was not a church-goer, he smoked and was Scottish. She valued his ability to 'fix things' even if she didn't understand his frustrations nor many of his ideas. 'Ask your father,' was her answer to any questions and she was proud of his general knowledge. In an era where a female's status was determined by being married, she was proud to be a Mrs and have a family.

Hazel's parents: David and Grace Muir Moir

They were genuinely fond of each other as a couple, even though complete opposites. Her name was Hazel Grace, but she was known as Grace and he suggested using one of her names for baby me. Luckily they settled on Hazel, as neither my mother nor I were graceful. My mother was known for 'putting her foot in it', a characteristic which I may have inherited although geneticists claim there is no gene for tact or the lack of it.

My mother once told me they didn't intend having a child. A disillusioned socialist after the economic depression of the thirties, my father thought it unfair to bring a child into an unsafe world during WW2, but I was born in 1945, regardless.

My middle name, 'Eileen', was the name of two of my mother's friends and each claimed the honour. Our surname was always a challenge: Muir Moir. Apparently Gaelic for 'big'. We tended to use only Moir, unless on official documents. This was before the hyphenated names of children of blended families or mothers retaining their professional surnames. I mistakenly assumed there must have been a second marriage or a stepmother to provide the double surname. Only after my father's death did we discover that Muir had been his mother's maiden surname, and the common Scottish practice of retaining this as a middle name.

In adulthood, this mysterious paternal grandmother Agnes intrigued me, because an old photo revealed we had the same face. And maybe a few other attributes.

Scottish Ancestors

Writing Names and Pseudonyms That Didn't Work

I wasn't book-published until after I was married at 21, and so used Edwards as my writing name. That 'moved me up the alphabet from M to E' next to Dahl (Roald) and Earls (Nick), just at eye level on the bookshelves, instead of knee-level at the M shelf. Irrelevant for picture books which were shelved according to illustrator, and since I worked with several, my picture books were all over the place.

A few authors have multiple writing names, as there is a benefit in matching a name to a genre when readers have specific expectations of that type of book.

My venture into a pseudonym for crime writing as Davina Muir Moir was a disaster. The banks had suffered a 'bottom of the harbour' financial scandal and were obsessive about bank names matching real people and no phantom bank accounts with dodgy aliases. When I went to arrange if any cheque paid for a published story by Davina Muir Moir could be paid into my Edwards account, the official bank forms were endless. Irony was, I never sold that story and didn't earn any money from it which needed banking. Also Known As (A.K. Aye.) as part of the four-woman group-writing adult mystery 'Formula for Murder' is my only official pseudonym. This was our way of acknowledging all four writers on the cover.

Collaborators

Many friends became collaborators on creative projects. Or maybe it was the other way around, as social life and work merged. Teaching was the obvious choice for females wanting an education, because of the studentship which was comparable to first-year wages in banks or insurance companies, the usual destination for students if you didn't go nursing. Often my contemporaries were the first generation in their family going to university, frequently as part-timers or at night after a full day's work. The sequence from teacher to author, adult trainer or educational psychologist and to various small businesses based on intellectual property was a natural progression. I was always attracted to energetic personalities and these were often the innovators who had overlapping skills and several changes of occupation.

Being a freelancer with a home office meant family was entwined and I worked with other educator–authors in comparable circumstances. The Clarke family had parallel-aged children, and shared some projects as educator–publishers as well as playing sport, sharing theatre or concert tickets or travelling together. There was less stress when friends had similar commitments and a social life was flexible around the working hours of the self-employed. The Clarkes' process of their mud brick home was also inspiration for the *Oinkabella* picture book story setting.

I remember weekends at the beach to finish a book with a co-author where we played exhausting games with the four children (two each) to wear them out, simultaneously talking through the book's structure, then worked into the night on our project once the children slept. Or speaking at a regional conference, and taking the one paid babysitter to look after the children of both families.

'Aren't you lucky to get a book published,' was a comment. 'Nice hobby.'

She's Got My Face!

I didn't want to get the family history bug, but ... one ancestor intrigued me. We're look-alikes. Two generations apart. Agnes Muir Moir, my paternal grandmother.

As a mystery writer, clues interest me, and here was a structure of motivations I didn't have to create: the personalities were already there, and so I just had to uncover the name clues.

- My father David Muir Moir left Glasgow in 1926, for Australia and adventure, aged 20, and never returned.
- He never spoke about his parents; papers found only after his death gave a Glasgow address.

And that's what intrigued me about Granny Agnes: the inconsistencies in her story. A widow with seven children, who lived in Glasgow and yet she travelled to Russia, the Mediterranean,

USA and Switzerland. Her son David, my father, read political philosophy and played the violin at home. He tried to teach me violin as a child, but my screechy noises alienated everybody. I persisted for a few months because violin practice was a valid excuse for avoiding my job of doing the dishes.

In 1984, Garnet and I went to Europe with our children aged 8 and 11 and had one day in Glasgow to devote to finding Muir Moir family history clues. *Facing Secrets* was written soon after, so I wouldn't forget the details.

Facing Secrets

My dad's past was a secret. So it became mine.

Since my father wouldn't answer questions about his childhood, I imagined the worst. Disinherited royalty? A wicked stepmother? Prison? Espionage? A family Black Sheep pensioned to 'the colonies'? We had no money, so he couldn't have been paid to stay away.

As a child, when I was 'in trouble', I imagined that I was really the secret offspring of royal, famous, or at least wealthy Scottish ancestors.

Since he spoke with a broad Glaswegian accent, served porridge with salt and quoted the Scots poet Robbie Burns, it was no secret that he was born in Scotland.

Although he used the Socratic method of asking questions until I found my own answers, whenever I got the courage to ask about his past, he'd only say, 'Better here than in the Gorbals,' which he always said were the slums of Glasgow where he grew up. (Later a relative disputed this, saying they did not live in the slums.)

My parents had met and married in Melbourne where my Dad was holidaying after gold prospecting in the outback for years. Internationally, the Salvation Army operate a 'Missing Persons' service, and when I was five, they tracked my father to our Melbourne home. Reassured he was alive, they left.

A Scottish doll arrived from Aunty Jean for 'wee Hazel'. First we knew Dad had a sister.

A believer in equality, he brought me up as a girl–boy, encouraging me to play sport, read widely, treat millionaires and workers equally and not be afraid of being different. But there were no photos of his past. After my father died in 1970, my mother found a Scottish address in his papers, and sent a message by snail mail.

In 1984, with a day in Glasgow, we decided to track my father's past. No luck with the phone book. Then two addresses. 6 Redan Street and Dumcross Road, no number. It was a shock to discover that Redan Street no longer existed. Slum clearance of the 'Gorbals' had wiped out the entire block. Dumcross turned out to be a long road, so we decided to try houses with good gardens. More chance of an avid gardener noticing neighbours.

'D'you know anyone by the name of …' we asked the owner of the best garden.

'Yes. But she died three months ago.'

My heart sank. So close.

'But Jean's daughter is there,' continued the gardener. 'Why don't you ask her?'

I walked up the path rehearsing, 'Hullo. My name is Hazel. I'm from Australia. My father was David. I think I'm your cousin.'

I knocked.

The woman who opened the door looked like me.

Obviously she got a shock too.

'My name is Moira,' she said.

A definite family link to Muir Moir.

We met the clan at afternoon tea. Aunt 'Nessie' (same Agnes name, different generation), the current matriarch in her seventies, sat surrounded by family whom she introduced, adding, 'And then there's Robert who went to Australia. Have you seen him?'

'No. Australia is quite big.'

Then I was interrogated, which is not too strong a term for

the questioning. My handicap was I married the enemy ... an Englishman who was keeping very quiet that day.

'Do you drink?'
'What?'
'Do you drink whisky?'
'No.'
'Are you religious?'
'No.'
'What do you do?'
'Write books.'
'Mmm.'

Author was just acceptable.

'Excuse me Nessie ... Could I ask you a few questions about my father, David?'

'Ask me?'

1967 Wedding of Hazel & Garnet

Obviously it was a novelty for locals or family to challenge Nessie's control of the conversation. But by the end of the afternoon, there was mutual acceptance and admiration. I admired her feisty spirit, even if we were different generations.

They talked of fiery, political activist David as a beloved, intelligent but erratic 20-year-old who had gone overseas after a protest 'incident' during the Depression when he'd nearly been arrested. He left to make his fortune in order to help his family. No money and misplaced pride stopped him from returning despite sporadic exchanges of letters with his mother. A time warp, because I was remembering the same man in his sixties.

Cousin 'Robert' turned out to live in my Australian suburb, only three streets away! That's one geographic coincidence I'd never use in fiction. Months later, a package of old letters in my father's copperplate, addressed to his mother decades earlier, arrived from Scotland recycled for 'David's daughter', on the day my 21-year-old son left to backpack around Australia. A photo of my father at the same age fell out of the pile. Same body. Same sandy colouring.

Why start the 'Granny Agnes' research again, years later?

My husband Garnet subscribed to Ancestry.com to find the ancestors of his distinctively named Welsh mother, Mary Jane Jones. He did! And with a friend's help, found his 'Uncle' Garnet amongst the WWI military records.

Military history was well documented. We also found my grandfather Alexander Moir's WWI military cemetery grave in France. This was the husband of 'my' Granny Agnes.

In 1918, Agnes Muir Moir was left a widow with her seven children to care for. It appears that Agnes inherited some property from her father, and bought into the Gorbals in the more upmarket Bridgeton to support her children. She was not a money-lender nor pawnbroker as first hinted. (That appealed to the storyteller in me). She was still a strong female who'd lost a husband and several sons within a short period and I'd like to learn more of her. I was concerned how her teenage sons might have died, and whether either had been suicide, but one was a railway accident and the other a heart problem. She must have had great resilience to cope with such losses. Maybe Agnes could become the basis of a factional story set in that period?

As I get older, I'm more inclined to believe that genetic inheritance is dominant rather than nurture, and maybe that's a worry? Legacies can be mixed, but also affected by the external variables of economic hardship or war. Or times of good fortune and opportunity too. I've been so privileged to have educational opportunities to gain skills in a period of peace and prosperity and become a writer. There's always a gap between aspiration and reality. If my father had been born in my times, what might have been different?

Legacies

My father committed suicide. He died on April 1st. I was 24. He was 63. I am now older than he was when he died.

As a writer, I'm aware of the need for dramatic openings. Juxtaposing suicide and April Fools' Day certainly does that. But I'm also aware that there are some subjects about which I have preferred not to write. Suicide is one.

And yet, maybe it is important for therapeutic reasons for myself and for others.

I do not regard suicide as failure. Nor as a disgrace. Much depends upon the individual and why that choice was made. For someone who is profoundly depressed, maybe they would have made a different choice at another time. To a certain extent, I understand why my father made a 'rational' decision to end his life. He was suffering from cerebral sclerosis, a kind of deterioration of the brain which affected his balance. He'd been a physically strong man, and didn't want to deteriorate further. So he decided he'd had enough.

There were also financial problems, since he couldn't work.

He was an intelligent man, and perceptive enough to realise

the ironic significance of the date and may even have chosen it deliberately.

Why have I chosen to write about suicide now?

There's been emphasis upon mental health issues in the media. Suddenly family history searches re-open earlier attitudes to suicide which was 'hushed up' or regarded as a disgrace.

My mother felt that way too. Suicides used to be buried outside the churchyard walls. Death insurance was not paid to families of members who took their own lives. Further hardship.

The real issue with suicide is the method and implications for those left behind. Legal. Emotional. Financial. And genetic.

My father shot himself. There was an inquest. And there were difficult times where a twenty-something daughter had to become parent to the mother. To respond to a phone call from the police station to come and collect the gun. To identify the body. To find the note to prove it was not murder. To deal with a funeral, where the Protestant clergyman was struggling to say something innocuous about a man who had been an agnostic. And whom he had never met before, except at the daughter's wedding.

Because I've been writing about family history, I've used some of my father's adventurous stories as anecdotes in my work, and ironically, in articles and books, he 'lives on', internationally, for his earlier strengths, in a way he would never have predicted.

What has been the impact of his suicide on me, as his only child and the one who carries his genes? Including the depressive DNA?

At times, I worry whether any descendant will also carry his melancholia. How much is nurture and how much nature?

My heart goes out to families who lose a child to suicide, at any age. Adolescent years can distort worries but a man in his sixties is responsible for his own decisions.

But I also question some definitions of mental health or the lack of it. Maybe things just 'are' and labelling causes more anguish rather than providing strategies for those remaining or who have to cope on a daily basis.

The legacies my father left me were an inquiring mind, physical and intellectual risk taking and the expectation that you had to work hard, but that it was OK to be different. A good legacy.

Hazel's father David

CHAPTER 14
DOMESTIC SURVIVAL?

Being a Parent and a Writer

How can you have a partner, a family, a job, and write?
 Quality writing and quality parenting are abstractions which you can't measure. And so is good teaching. When have you done enough? And if you haven't got it right at the crucial time, will opportunities be missed later? You are never sure. Are you a good partner and a good friend? That's subjective and depends upon their needs. Do you contribute to the wider community or is your writing self-indulgent introspection?
 I knew I wanted to be a writer but was unsure how to juggle family time and responsibilities. I married at 21, taught secondary school and lectured at teachers' college, studying at night at university, and had my first child at 27. While our children were babies, I taught weird versions of part-time, or concentrated workshops mainly at night and weekends. My widowed mother willingly helped with emergency babysitting if a child was sick at 7 a.m., although she didn't drive and had to be picked up. She enjoyed coming with me to country talks, where I spoke for an hour, while she looked after the children and then we had a family outing. I was also guardian for my disabled cousin and his blind but resourceful mother Violet, who was my favourite aunt. There was little advice around on juggling those roles. Most writers were single, in short-term relationships, or were male.
 Full-time mothers had flexible schedules and no money. Professional women had money and no time. Female authors had neither.
 Male writers had wives to support their literary ambition and publicise their works while providing domestic back-up. It

was acceptable for males to write as an occupation. But if you were female, how could you have a partner, a family, a job, and write? My decision was to try.

Before we married, Garnet and I had agreed on an unusual arrangement for that time. We would share the parenting and other roles and have dual careers. That was most unusual in the late 1960s and 70s. And I pay Garnet credit for the way he coped, as he was managing a hospital, and studying, as well as being willing to change pooey nappies. We had one car and a mortgage and lots of bookshelves. Our house was simply designed for easy care. Neither of us were keen gardeners (most plants died under our care), but we did have friends around for thematic Murder dinner parties and Witty Women's Lunches, included the children in our activities, travelled as a family and had fun.

As I taught regular night classes, we'd have a split-second–timed 'hand-over of baby and car and say Pureed apples'. I remember parking illegally in a city churchyard at 5.55 p.m. to hand over, as Garnet was working in the city and I had a night class. Nearly got booked that time.

I was lucky as part of the post-WW2 Baby Boomers bulge of the population which meant that whatever was happening to me was happening to other families. So I wrote short funny stuff about 'change' at a time when the perception of female roles was changing radically. Using humour was one way of exploring sociological change like the superwoman myth or female mature-aged students.

Domestic Time Management?

Time management was a big issue for parents working outside the home—as was child-care. And breaking into the literary world was an even bigger gamble. I kept the rejection slip from a major publisher which said 'We don't publish fiction,' when I offered a satirical manuscript on domestic time-management hints based on interviews and my workshop manual. Years later it was published and reprinted as *Houseworking: the Unsuperperson's Guide to Sharing the Load.* Just had my timing wrong, but indicative of the prevailing 1970s attitude towards women with families who worked outside the home. Issues were seen as moral rather than economics and time management. I'd read Germaine Greer and Betty Friedan, but my solution was just to get on with my own version of suburban feminism, by tutoring women who returned to study.

Put-downs make it hard to persist when there's no proof of publication or income. How do you get the headspace to write when some adults dismissively call it 'your little hobby of writing for the little kiddiwinks' or 'Kidlit' which sounds like kitty litter?

I had my first novel published in the same year as my first child was born. I was slowly studying for a Masters degree (which I called my Mistress degree), teaching in suburban adult groups, and writing. I felt guilty about the time allocated to my writing in comparison with study time, which had a career purpose. It's said that mothers always find something to feel guilty about. That's the problem with intangibles. What do you say to the inevitable, polite question?

'What are you working on now?'

Or, 'Are you writing anything at present?'

Yes. I was always writing concurrent projects. But the success rate was about 1%.

I was lucky that my third publication was the picture book *There's a Hippopotamus on our Roof Eating Cake,* which gave me an author credit, especially as it went into translations and sold internationally.

You need to act like a professional author, and judge the role by output and quality and effect on readers, not necessarily income. I was 'acting' for a few years.

Five Year Apprenticeship?

I wrote when I could, and regarded that time as my five-year apprenticeship since most projects were rejected and little published. Then I became more realistic and looked at potential markets for the skills I had. As a trained teacher and a less-than-perfect mother of young children and woeful housekeeper, it made sense to write about what I was experiencing, so I began regarding parenting as research, and wrote funny 'how to' journalism, or used mishaps like birthday parties gone wrong or family sport as story settings. I didn't regard writing about children or being a children's author as a lesser craft than writing about psychology or history, it was just shorter and more manageable since I was living the participation–observation research.

So my 'how to' books like *Women Returning to Study* or *Writing a Non-Boring Family History* were sociological observations with humour and survival hints, started as workshop manuals because others were experiencing similar challenges and a readership existed. Brief satires were also manageable as I could plot while doing routine domesticity or in the car between sporting pick-ups. Most of my longer books were compilations of interviews or articles, or anthologies which re-used already published shorter works. Impatient but persistent, I prefer shorter projects.

My second strategy was to use subjects in more than one way, and then write about the process for the educational market. Double value. This included classroom performance scripts linked to the picture books and later the stage productions and animation.

The big challenge is finding the physical time to write. So you tend to say 'No' to social occasions and that's a mistake. Often the anecdotes you hear at local chats with neighbours, friends and family keeps your writing in perspective.

How did we manage?

Less Sleep

I learnt to manage on less sleep; by not remembering how few hours I slept. It was really hard when feeding babies and I used to move in a fog. I preferred to write into the night to finish a story.

Consolidating geographically saved lots of time across the years. A home office, schools within walking, local suburban classes, and neighbouring babysitter helped. Inviting colleagues to meet at my home. That was the ideal. The reality was a bit more haphazard.

We moved to our current house because the babysitter lived a block away. Then she moved!

'Where do you live?' my 3-year-old daughter was asked.

'At the crèche.'

True for Thursdays which was my concentrated writing day. Later both children had full-day kindergarten. And I was grateful that Garnet budgeted time when there was no obvious financial return from my writing. When starting out with few or no writing credits and only costs, not income, it's an act of faith to 'invest' from a couple's limited income. I loved a colleague's feisty story about papering the toilet door with multi-coloured rejection slips. Interior decorating or recycling?

I wrote in concentrated bursts. Near the end of a book, I'd need an uninterrupted block to link layers together. It took effort to get that story written instead of 'vegging out' in front of television. It was hard to delete if not good enough.

Occasionally you know something is good and there's a rhythm to the creative parts fitting together like a fractal pattern. I always knew the cake-eating hippo story was good. Years later, I felt the same way about *f2m: the boy within* as a coming of age characterisation, especially as we were the first to tackle a novel on transitioning gender with a co-author who was an ftm (female to male). There were rhythmic layers. As co-authors we just had to get them structured in an accessible way for others to experience. Maintaining confidence in your literary projects or even your own ability is hard, but occasionally you 'know' that an idea has the right shape.

1970s acquaintances criticised me for spending time on 'a paid job' as a wife and mother, so unpaid writing, seen as selfish, was worse. 'A nice hobby' was just acceptable, and only after you'd ironed the pillow cases. I didn't iron anything. Drip dry was vital for a minimalist household. I started avoiding social lunches where the domestic critics gathered and tried to socialize with like-minded people so I wouldn't go home depressed.

A few international writers are disparaging about running 'creative writing' classes and the value to the students of such courses. I found being the tutor forced me to analyse techniques. Not sure about 'creative' in the class title as that implies non-fiction cannot be creative. Wrong. Often I'd take a problem from a manuscript as the example. Maybe some would see this as unprofessional, but it was realistic. I was learning 'on the job' too which wasn't such a bad role model for other adult students who had families, jobs and little spare time or money, unlike many of the authors we studied, like Virginia Woolf's 'A Room of One's Own' and need for an income of 500 a year. Woolf came from a privileged Bloomsbury background and her husband owned the publishing house, but her ideas inspired others.

In class, we'd work out approaches to solving problems whether dialogue, viewpoint, titles, tense or something more basic like what was the subject and was it worth writing. The cross-usage of the writing and teaching was a survival skill in time and energy, but also playing with ideas. I loved discussions with my adult students who were nominally studying a certificate course, but we were operating at university level in the proper sense of extending ideas into 'What if?' abstractions.

Literature was an apt course for those exploring their changing roles and entering the fictional worlds of other possibilities or philosophies. That was also why I liked sharing biographies of writers like Simone de Beauvoir or George Orwell to learn how they learnt. Often artists or thinkers fringed on the literary world. We also reviewed the over-rated. Where no-one is prepared to say that the introspective poetic novel in stream of consciousness with no punctuation, which you've spent so long studying, wasn't worth it, despite what fashionable critics say.

Sometimes I don't know the answers or even the problem until I talk or write it through and capture the abstraction in words. Occasionally I'd find there was an official term for the amorphous thought and realise I already knew that, but didn't know the terminology in that discipline. Co-writing helped me. Psychology was studded with motivations for characters, and often I knew what a character needed to do, but hadn't known psychologists called that obsessive-compulsive or narcissism. Authors often 'know' how to create relationships for characters, and psychologists know the labels and identify categories.

Another dilemma was how to present professionally, with babies in tow. Anticipatory anxiety about noisy children during recorded interviews worried me. Inevitably if there was a TV or radio phone interview, that's when the baby would cry or the toddler have a tantrum. Or the neighbour mow his lawn, loudly. On the day the first TV crew filmed at our home, I was conscious of the dust when they moved the furniture and I'd never noticed those windows needed cleaning. So I decided it was better to be authentic in public, rather than hypocritically perfect. Audiences and readers identify with fallible honesty. We all have weaknesses.

Upskill Family

I used to review children's books for a newspaper, and my kids loved access to new books and meeting the authors and illustrators. I'm ashamed to admit I also 'bribed' with an ice cream or milkshake after they helped me photocopy or scan documents. So they associated work with reward.

Family holidays included finding out about settings for stories, and they became more observant travellers. Kim became our photographer because I always chopped legs off subjects and visually she was the best at setting up a photo shoot.

Gourmet cooking lessons as birthday gifts ensure all can cook, especially the males. But meals need to be followed with on-going praise. Computer gaming addicts can operate the washing machine or dish-washer if you present it as a challenge. (That's the theory but not always the practice.)

85% Compromise

85% achieved may be better than not even attempting the project.

CHAPTER 15
MENTORING, MINTEES AND HAZELNUTS

**Did you always want to be a writer?
Did you have a mentor?**

The short answer is yes, to both questions.

I wanted to be an author from aged six.

I'd never met a writer personally until I was 23 and shared a cupboard–office at Frankston Teachers' College with a charismatic educator who was also internationally published. George Pappas was the first 'real' author whose workstyle I could observe. Even now I'm wary of using 'real' and go quiet when I am introduced by well meaning hosts as 'A real live author', considering the alternative.

I enjoyed reading biographies of literary female lifestyles in my teens, but they all lived in Europe and had wealthy parents or multiple lovers. Later I read about Australians Charmian Clift, Miles Franklin, Nettie Palmer, Ruth Park, Mary Grant Bruce and Dame Mary Gilmore. Those married to writers seemed to do 'hack work' to support the loftier literary work of their partner. Less than ideal. If you wanted to be a writer, it seemed marriage was out.

'Being a writer' was always my aim, but I lacked role models of women artists who could combine family life and sustained literary work and the breadth of experience I imagined was essential outside suburbia or country Victoria. So meeting George was a start, in creative time management, even if he didn't have children, lived alone and was male.

Alice Springs: Yamba, the Honey Ant's T.V. program

George co-authored big-selling drama textbooks, but his life was the real drama. Officially, his 'day-job' was as a lecturer in drama to primary trainee teachers. A master teacher, he also produced and directed large-scale theatrical productions with trainees, as well as doing commercial voice-overs, co-scripting and television acting.

George mentored many young people and lived life crammed into 24-hour days. Not driver-licensed, as he loved the bonus of talking with the 'chauffeur'. He would 'crash' periodically. In bed, not crash the car! You wouldn't see him for several days and then he'd reappear, refreshed. George also taught the creative's timetable could work differently from bureaucrats' and was partly the reason I became self-employed and also unemployable.

'Have one of these.' George would hand me chocolate covered gingers.

I don't like ginger, but I liked George's mentoring and ate them as a peace offering. The first of many adaptations to be in the company of an interesting mind.

Who else would have a head of Egyptian Queen Nefertiti in

his suburban house entrance, use a photocopier instead of a kitchen table and have bookshelves across all walls, even his doorways. Visitors slipped a clip under the Egyptology shelf in order to enter the bedroom and leave their coats on the bed.

'Get married and have children,' George advised. He was a bachelor until his fifties, when he married a psychiatrist and they maintained separate book-lined households, commuting by taxi at weekends as neither drove. I was already married but knew that having children would curtail writing time and energy. I didn't anticipate family would provide writing inspiration and emotional support.

I liked to read about writers' lives.

As a child, I surreptitiously read under the bedclothes with a torch and later I started my lifelong reading-in-the-bath habit, adding more hot water if the plot were engrossing. Aqua-readaholic was a term I later started using when asked about my 'bad' habits. But not with e-books in the bath as I might 'fuse' myself.

I'd buy the *School Friend* magazines, which had a very English boarding school emphasis which was a long way from my 'real life'.

My mother read Mills and Boon romances. My father read philosophy and worked his way through the major thinkers. In between he read the horse racing guide. My librarian grandfather read volumes of *The Decline and Fall of the Roman Empire* in between planning his sermons as a lay preacher. When he'd finish, he went back to the beginning. It was he who started me on espionage and mystery novels like Agatha Christie after I finished the children's section. Apart from the Bible, my Grandma read me Sunday School Prize books, which had strongly didactic messages about 'being good'.

When my children were teenagers, George's biographer contacted me, wanting to interview me. His questions brought back memories and gratitude for my first writing 'mentor'.

George's funeral was private and friends found out about his death later. We had a 'wake' telling 'George' stories like: when he withdrew a sheaf of large denomination bank notes, and while he was crossing the highway they blew away!

So that's the 'long answer' to 'Did you always want to be a writer?'

On the Red Carpet

Mintee

'Mintee' is the affectionate name for those who are mentored, but I have a group of self-named 'Hazelnuts' whom I have mentored into publication. Now the majority have been mainstream or indie published and each help workshop and launch the others' work. I've also collaborated on various fiction and factual books and help 'genis' writing their non-boring family histories. Important to capture the extraordinary behind the so-called ordinary lives.

A Bunch of Hazelnuts! How many of your writing students got published?

Working with adult students has provided some of the greatest satisfactions for me. I taught suburban Council of Adult Education classes when my children were small and later lectured sessionally at Holmesglen TAFE's Diploma of Professional Writing.

This is the foreword I wrote for my students' book 'A Bunch of Hazelnuts'.

All adult writing classes are different. Chances are you'll have experts from varied fields, and that's the delight. We all learn together. Classmates include engineers, rap musicians, truckies, hairdressers, potters, gardeners, singers, psychologists, nannies, herbalists, actors, speech pathologists, teachers, parents, chemists, check-out chicks and roosters, interpreters, illustrators, and I've even had an ex-spy in an earlier class. Many speak and write multiple languages.

It just so happens that my skills are in crafting ideas in accessible English and anecdultery (structuring mini stories with humour).

Age, shape, gender or culture doesn't matter, except in the first five minutes in the opening class, and in providing perspectives and facts from which to write.

My adult students are aware of my deficiencies in formatting and filling in rolls. But I hope they gain a realistic insight into the workstyle of a professional creator.

Hazelnuts

Librarian Ozge & illustrator Ann James

More Hazelnuts

Most people who enrol for a year-long writing project course have a subject about which they are passionate. Their content matters. They have 'real' experience of value to others in our society. They just need help writing it.

Often 'tragic' historical material needs to be crafted so the writer can make sense of a past, but the reader is not overwhelmed and rejects the story.

Common strands are those who wish to write aspects of their family history for grandkids or to make sense of their migrant or refugee parents' earlier struggles. Others want to write 'How to ...' books in their specialties, such as health, cooking or racing. Some plan autobiographies but often settle on 'memoirs' focusing on important stages.

Writing is more than therapy. An amateur writes for the love of writing and for himself or herself as the only reader (or maybe their Mum). A professional invests time to craft those ideas and experiences in a format more people will read, so it's effective use of time, both ways.

National Reading Ambassadors: Tania McCartney & Dr. Anita Heiss

As a self-employed author, I encouraged habits which would enable creators to work regularly and to a high standard, but also to get recognition for their efforts. We 'celebrated' acceptance, publication or awards with a champagne, or even an 'imaginary' toast. Networking was encouraged, beyond the class, so that those with a significant story to tell about extraordinary so-called ordinary people could do so.

I enjoy seeing the 'light bulb' moment when an adult student understands.

As a mentor, I consider that I am 'giving back' in practical ways from the viewpoint of a practitioner, not an academic dealing only in theory. I'm also an authorpreneur, aware of the need for an artist to learn media skills and to initiate paid work.

TAFEs, and for the older age group U3A University of the Third Age, offer 'a second chance' to those who wish to learn new skills.

A writing tutor's role is to offer technical suggestions, and set up a workshopping environment in which people's stories can be crafted for a wider audience. The rest of the class creates the public opinion responses, which may differ, enabling 'testing' of those ideas.

Commercial publication is not the only aim, but on average 3–4 books are published by major publishers within a couple of years of those students completing their year-long course. Others find their aims change. Completing the writing of a book-length project is a creative achievement, inspiring the confidence to tackle other goals.

Many ex-students retain contact, because friendships have been formed from the depth of ideas explored, or from new socialising via galleries, book launches and festival attendance. Lives have been deepened because others' motivations are better understood.

An ex-student, now a published author and exhibited artist, told me that a 'filbert' is a cultured hazel nut, and maybe that could be my pseudonym. A freelance filbert? A bunch of filberts doesn't have the same ambiguity of title, but ...

Titles are vital. I am proud that my students are choosing among 'A Bunch of Hazelnuts', 'A Hazelnuts Collection', or even colloquially the 'Hazelnits'. Playing with words works.

CHAPTER 16
MYSTERY WRITING ON LOCATION

Why Mysteries?

I started writing mysteries to improve my plotting, to develop series and enable me to travel with a purpose, which suited my workaholic conscience. The Frequent Flyer Twins, set in various airports, were my first junior sleuths: 10-year-old Asian–Australian sister and brother problem-solvers, followed later by Astrid, a hi-tech mind-reading chook who rode a Harley. Sleuth characters needed to be versatile enough to move into different settings enabling each book to have a different focus, and for me to explore a new subject, setting or occupation, but not a violent crime.

So the frequent flyer twins were involved in artnapping, smuggled wildlife and fake brand mysteries. Sleuth Astrid became involved with football when the coach lost his voice before the grand final. And I learnt about new worlds, like Aussie Rules obsessive loyalties to footy codes and the difference between a referee and an umpire.

In between, I wrote short adult crime mysteries which utilised settings such as gourmet barging on the French canals or 'rambling' in the Cotswolds, complete with clotted cream teas. Food is the sex of children's fiction but I included other appetites in my adult fiction. I realised that obsession was a strong motive for crime.

My adult stories involved psychological manipulation of characters. Writing from the viewpoint of a controlling 'I' personality who committed the deed was a challenge. Researching 'sociopaths' for our factual *Difficult Personalities* carried over into the fiction of this period.

I'd always been interested in motivations which were different, but single-minded 'sociopaths' who considered themselves blameless, and had no anticipatory anxiety because they always knew they were right, were easier to write than my heroes. That was a worry. These were complicated plots where the dates and timing mattered, so I started using charts and maps. Despite this, I needed editorial help on final versions to ensure I hadn't jumped a few days on the concentrated time line or had my sleuth and suspects in the wrong place on the wrong day.

Stalker, my Young Adult novel, was written from dual viewpoints, and the obsessive stalker was easier for me to write than the stalked heroine, who was a voluntary presenter on community radio. But I had to check the stalker's location for every scene, so the later 'twist' would be plausible.

The setting of *Stalker* was a fictitious community radio station, BC (which I named by dropping the A from ABC radio). I was familiar with the roles of panel operator and presenter as well as challenges in being a guest talking alone in box-like studios with the interviewer elsewhere. Ironically I was later interviewed at the real Brisbane 4BC radio station about my fictitious character Lily being stalked in fictional BC radio station. And the 'real' 4BC interviewer confessed they'd all suffered from stalkers but tended to keep quiet about obsessional fans to discourage others, and had I really been stalked myself?

Either I'd immerse myself in a setting and hope to find some authentic inconsistency which could be used in a mystery or else I'd visit to find out 'What might go wrong around here?' That could make you unpopular with officious staff who ran their workplaces perfectly and who got upset about hypothetical crimes in their settings. When I asked the local swimming pool management how the sauna door could be wedged to murder an over-hot client, and how long it would take, they were not amused.

Later came invitations to run international writing workshops which utilised local settings and which were problem-solving exercises. So cluey plotting has occurred in museums, historic pubs and art galleries: anywhere with a bit of history to enable past, present and future and lots of entrances and exits for characters. Adults and younger writers enjoy mystery plotting, especially in groups, and I like 'thinking on the spot' plotting. It's quite sociable and yet factual. Apprentice script writers acted out the scenes which led to the embarrassing moment of a security guard at a university bio-lab thinking the anti–animal house protesters were real, not characters in a mystery enactment.

'Hey, you can't do that!'

Almost arrested by security that time.

Performing on site gives realistic feedback and is the last draft stage on location when you check if it's feasible for the character to do that, there. Each class at Blackburn Lake primary school wrote their own mysteries set around a real feature of the lake, such as the jetty, and then performed the finished story there, as the launch. Others at the Museum of South Australia did the same, but their storytelling was in front of specific exhibits like fossils. Outside is riskier. Of course things go wrong, like rainy weather.

Like the full-scale, 170-student–cast, outside performance of *Voice of the Forest* at Wilson's Promontory with rain and choppers interrupting. Earlier, after a term's rehearsal, the entire school had performed at dusk, on their school oval, the eco-play which has numerous wildlife choruses and which linked with their curriculum study for that term. I wrote the original script, but they added local ideas such as pretend 'virtual reality glasses' for the audience to cope with the difference in size of the Eucalypt Gum tree actor and the bees' chorus. Audience pretended to don these glasses as they entered through a flower-festooned gateway on the oval grass. Wilson's Prom was a requested extra performance for the public.

Frankly I learnt a lot about trees and bugs doing that play.

And the schoolgirl who played the 'Dung Beetle' both times

was memorable. Even her estranged father turned up to watch his daughter perform, a significant first for her. He was SO proud. Nothing quite like watching the audience, as well as the cast, when your script is performed. Love the atmosphere when parents and friends help 'dress up' the characters, clap regardless of mishaps and then cheer when they realise that the performance is actually good and they can relax. Or watching burly farmer–Dads try to attach bee-wings to tiny, wriggling, over-excited students.

Seeing one of my scripts performed is the most wonderful feedback when used to creating in isolation. The 'atmosphere' added during performances is electric.

Another school had a 'Hippo-fest' where each class performed one of the classroom scripts related to the hippo picture books for the younger students. It was just acceptable to perform because it was for the younger 'prep' buddies, but really the older students had more fun. Literacy and 'Buddies' in action, because there's a reason for reading. Often the sound effects expert is a non-reader who converts to reading via the set instructions. If you need to be able to read to make the play work, they do.

At one stage there was a possibility my Frequent Flyer Twins would be turned into a 13-part TV series. I had to find 13 reasons why a plane might be grounded so my 10-year-old twin sleuths could investigate a mystery. That filled in a bit of dead time at airports.

Even when there's lots of sitting and waiting in transit, I regard it as people-research and chat up the next passenger. I've learnt about plastic corks on wine bottles from the salesman, and about electronic surveillance in prisons which was timely for my *Stalker* novel. Learning that some international musicians buy a plane seat for their instruments and then have to provide a passenger name for the boarding pass of Mr G (the guitar), who then lacks baggage, which can be a security problem and became a clue in my mystery.

French barge research

Sentenced

Why bother to visit a difficult-to-get-to location? One fact from visiting the place gives authenticity and provides a potential clue for a mystery. Often it's a smell or a phrase: the lack of smell in Antarctica (except for penguin poo) or the platitudes of pseudo philosophers at the casino who talk of 'investing' rather than gambling. Then local details which can be added to the plot: free airport umbrellas at humid Cairns because of tropical downpours, or thieving kia birds on the Milford Track who steal food or travellers' belongings left outside the hut doors. Or the strong female Nepali porters with headbanded heavy loads who wear thongs and incongruously labelled T-shirts like 'Boston Marathon' donated from former trekkers. Each occupation and job has its own vocabulary, and you must get that right. Like 'boffin' or 'tradies' in Antarctica.

If plotting non-violent mysteries, young writers pay more attention locally. And that has practical consequences. One shocked school principal repainted the entire college after students used the ultra-grey buildings as the setting for a mystery. That school planted a colourful vegetable and flower garden as a community project to counteract the 'grey'. Administration hadn't realised the surrounds were so depressing before. Thus fiction became fact. Not forgetting the university campus more aware of defects in their digital security when gifted students plotted a mystery around a missing student who never existed.

Collaborative mystery writing produces better plots because a second mind can query discrepancies of time, coincidences or unresolved 'red herrings'. And can ask 'Why?' a character would act in that way.

Munich's Castle of Books—for tolerance

Settings

Although not superstitious, there are three places I've been conscious of a brooding atmosphere of despair in the walls:

Fremantle Jail, Dachau concentration camp in Germany and the house of a well known writer who shall remain nameless. Tragic histories associated with settings do influence the atmosphere within a mystery.

'Where are you working now?'
'The jail.'
'What were you sentenced for?'
'Creativity.'

I was writer-in-residence at the old Fremantle Jail, which now contains the Children's Literature Centre. The former prison hospital had been turned into a gallery for children's book illustrations, thus creating an oasis of creativity inside grey walls.

Guest authors had a comfortable 'cell' in the residency, formerly an isolation ward. Artistically converted into a gallery, evidence of the former prison hospital remained in heavy padlocks, bars and the ever-encircling brick wall.

Twice daily, groups of children visited the displays of artwork featured in the former prison dispensary, operating room and ward space. Apart from the colour and delicacy of the artwork, and children's excited chattering, prison was still a bleak place. There's an irony in accommodating artists-in-residence, who tend to be highly sensitive to surroundings.

'Mystery Writing' workshops utilised the prison setting with a fictitious sleuth. In my workshops, dead bodies and violence are banned as too easy to write, and students were required to craft clues, motives, suspense and a believable twist at the end. In a prison setting, the challenge was to avoid the macabre violence that many wish to put into their stories, like the gallows at the end of our passageway.

Closed in 1991, the maximum security prison is now a tourist attraction. The hospital was separated from the major prison, with a veranda and a small herb garden. Ironically, rosemary—which symbolises remembrance—grows wild, and since the heritage garden had to be left with its combination of original plants, the rosemary remains. Perhaps a fictitious sleuth could be called Rosemary?

Late at night, the waves on Fremantle beach can be heard, even within the cells. Sound travels here, as I discovered when I let myself in at the watch tower, and the gate clanged behind me. Ahead were yellow spotlights lighting the walls and creating shadows around fences.

Noises. Creaks. Flutters. An owl on the veranda railing. Dusk and midnight $10 tours, with tiny torches provided, operated on Wednesday and Friday nights. Through my barred 'bedroom', I saw waving torches pinprick the dark.

Sleeping alone in a hospital prison cell is like being on an island.

'The safest place in Fremantle'—the director might have been right. Everything locked. The coiled barbed wire rattling above the exercise yard definitely exercised my imagination.

'Use the prison as a setting for your writing,' suggested the director.

Keys

Keys were the key. Students were given one minute to note ideas about the word 'key' as a clue. 'Keyhole', 'keyboard', 'car key (khaki)'. 'Could you have a sound key of any kind?' Yes, a keyboard. A musical key. A key answer. I issued an ambiguous word clue to each group of three. 'Net. Fork. Key. Ring.'

I avoided mentioning the suicide net above the first floor landing to prevent prisoners throwing over themselves or other objects.

Anecdotes, especially about animals, are useful when encouraging students to write. A young male boobook owl had been found clinging to a cross in the prison chapel that week. Perth Zoo birdkeepers using ladders and nets took 45 minutes to catch and release the owl, which they feared would starve inside.

This led into a discussion of viewpoint from which a story

could be told. The owl's viewpoint of a prison? The viewpoint of an inmate? A warder?

Later, I discovered from a tour guide that prisoners talked of the Gallows Owl which lived within the cellblock and probably fed on mice. In earlier times when a hanging was pending, if the owl flew to the north of the cellblock the man would be reprieved. If it flew to the south, he would be condemned.

I didn't mention this tall story to the students. Last night, there was a dark shape on the veranda outside my lighted but barred cell window. It was the owl.

Adventure Travel

With Garnet, I've tramped the four-day Milford Track including the zig-zag, puffing height to the Loo with a View, in New Zealand's South Island, to celebrate my 50th birthday but also to research *Fleeced*. At the same time an American adult crime writer was researching on the track too. It was fascinating to compare notes about what each of us intended using for our different readerships. At each hut was a log, and I noticed the American visitors reversed the day and month figures for dates, which could cause a possible clue. The 'celebrity' walker was a rugby player, and since rugby is a New Zealand religion, we both agreed on that clue. But certainly you walk more observantly if you know you're sending your characters along a real route, known to international readers.

Twists for the end?

Often, the ending may be added much later, because a mystery needs a really good twist. The plot has to be credible within that story, and a twist for the end may mean having to work backwards through the story to 'tweak' some earlier clues. Mysteries are often written backwards. Often my best ideas for endings come when swimming laps.

The Milford Track: participant research

CHAPTER 17
DO YOU PUT REAL PEOPLE IN YOUR STORIES?

'Do you put real people in your stories?'
'No.'

'Do people think you have written about them in your fiction?'
'Yes.'

'Have you?'
'Not exactly. A funny or weird incident with a real person may inspire a story. A character is always more complex and concentrated than any person in real life. I might 'borrow' a dramatic moment or authentic setting, but will always 'deepen' the motivations and increase the conflicts to make the story more involving for the reader. Or concentrate dramatic moments from several anecdotes into one person and a shorter time span.'

Even on an Antarctic voyage there are lots of quiet moments, it's not always high adventure with 'bergs, Patagonian Toothfish poachers or wildlife.

Writing characters for the *Antarctica's Frozen Chosen* novel was a different kind of challenge because expeditioners are known by their nicknames or their occupations, like Dieso (mechanic), Chippie, S.L. (Station leader) or Met-guy (meteorologist). And I decided to name my fictional characters by these roles too. On Australian Antarctic expeditions, most of the scientists can claim the title of Doc, but that's usually kept for the medical officer. During a Trivial Pursuit evening, teams were limited to 3 PhDs per team, despite the 'tradies' often out-answering the 'boffins' as the scientists were known. All excellent problem solvers who also helped me plot my novel, offering their expert knowledge.

So inevitably when my *Antarctica's Frozen Chosen* plot demanded a female station leader, many would assume I was writing about the real Marilyn on my Antarctic voyage, and that the other characters whom I called by their jobs would be based on fact. Well, their jobs were accurate, but the characters were made up.

Despite this, Critter, the real Dieso, always claimed that 'I'm a legend, Hazel. I'm on the cover of your *Antarctic Dad* and in the *Antarctica's Frozen Chosen* book.'

When I shared the draft, the others seemed pleased, rather than critical, at having their workstyles included in a novel. Very reassured by their positive responses, as I'd been nervous about their reactions and didn't want to imply I was taking over their stories.

When it's known that an author has been in a place, and then used it as a setting in a subsequent story, others assume it's autobiographical. Hard for murder mystery or romance writers.

Our children went to a local Jewish primary school, even though our family is not Jewish. And as the setting of *So Who's a Misfit*, later re-issued as *Misfit*, is a Jewish school with a non-Jewish girl as heroine, I knew it would be assumed the character Crystal was my daughter Kim and the story was autobiographical. Before the book was published, I checked with Kim. 'No problem Mum.'

One chapter was set during a birthday party mistakenly being held on a religious Yom Kippur day of fasting, and all the guests sent rejections. We rescheduled the birthday and all came. But it was an important scene in the book.

Although real people often inspire characters, the fictional ones are crafted. It's a bit insulting to suggest that a lazy author just 'pinched' from life, without crafting the motivations, conflicts and personality to deepen the story. Often the original inspiration may not have been aware of the significance of their contribution because it's been filtered through the imagination of the creator.

Animal antics are a different matter, and pet mishaps like dying goldfish, lost dogs or even irritating birds can be used as plot additions.

The only pet-owner who got upset that I had stolen the name and memories of his pet snake Axminster was completely wrong. Yes, I called the sequel to *Stickybeak* '*Axminster*' but that was because I heard of several snakes of that name, and it linked with the carpet brand. Yes, the disgruntled librarian owner did sit next to me at a literary dinner and tell me about his snake, but that was after the picture book text was drafted. A rare abusive letter which I didn't keep, but did heed the warning that not all readers feel it's a compliment to have their name in a book. Or that their personal interpretations are different from the writer's intention.

Vale Leila

Leila was my age. We met as 14-year-olds, when she worked in our general store. Leila inspired the character of Henrietta in my first novel, *General Store*, which was translated into Finnish.

When I hesitantly told her this, years later, she was pleased. By then, for me, there were three characters: the remembered, real, skinny 14-year-old girl Leila with black plaits; the real woman in her forties; and the 14-year-old, illiterate but resourceful character Henrietta whom I'd created. The 'fictional' character was the strongest one in my mind.

Like me, Leila was an only child. She marked time at primary school until the regulation leaving age of 14, and left.

Her parents had a small backblocks property but drove to Glengarry 'town', the four-shops-and-railway-station-and-pub, to buy their groceries on a Saturday and go to the local football in the afternoon.

Her tiny, muscular Dad worked on the roads for the council

and her Mum used to sit facing outwards in the back of their small open van. Leila knew the history and names of every local and helped my newcomer father in distinguishing those offspring with the three main surnames in the district.

My father offered her casual work, partly to help Leila's family and partly because in our 6-day-a-week store, we needed staff.

For two years, she bagged pollard, bran and sugar, pumped petrol, filled grocery orders and cheerfully did any manual jobs. She was scrupulously honest, had bad teeth, and the family didn't have a radio until my father helped her buy one. My mother also helped her 'get her teeth done', so at 15, Leila was proud of her full set of false teeth, and a perm paid for by her own work in the store.

In *General Store* the character Henrietta learned to read with help from Josie (not me). Leila could read, a bit. Character Josie learnt compassion from Henrietta and admiration for her resourcefulness. I did learn compassion from Leila. She was not envious, just interested in different lives from hers, which was just about everybody else.

Due to my father's need for an operation, we left the general store when I was 17 and moved to the city of Melbourne. Leila kept in touch. She'd send us clippings from the local newspaper about a few people I knew and others whom I increasingly had no idea who they were, but the surnames were vaguely familiar.

In between, Leila married cousin Colin and she sent me the wedding photo of her in a pink dress. 'Come and have a cuppa', was the invitation. I only visited her farm-home once. Not the best housekeeper in the world, we shared that trait, Leila was proud of her animals and home and was very welcoming. So was husband Colin.

And on the mantelpiece were several of my books, mainly unopened. I was touched that she collected them. Some I had posted to her, but others she'd tracked down. 'Lovely covers,' she'd say.

I'd send her autographed copies of my books or photos of

my growing family, and if I was speaking as an author in the area, I'd take her 'out for tea at the RSL', which was her choice.

When *There's a Hippopotamus on our Roof Eating Cake* was performed as a puppet play touring various theatres, I sent two front-row tickets for the nearby Warragul performance at the Gippsland Arts Centre.

She turned up in her best blue dress with look-alike relative.

'That was bloody beauty Hazel,' Leila boomed from one end of the theatre foyer.

The 'Beige Lady' front of house turned to me, 'Is that person with you?'

'Yes, Leila is a friend of mine,' I answered.

Leila didn't travel beyond a 100-kilometre radius. Sale or Warragul for medical appointments was about it, whereas I went on Antarctic expeditions, French barges and climbed the Great Wall of China. In our occasional chats, she'd just say, 'Marvellous.' And ask about my kids or grandkids, by name.

In later years, I'd get an occasional phone call, updating me on the latest medical test or that Colin had lost his driver's licence and couldn't get another one because he couldn't read the questions. That meant there was no legal driver in the household.

Putting these Leila anecdotes together implies we were in touch regularly, but that wasn't so. There were gaps of years in between, but I'd send her a Christmas letter.

Our last meeting was a 'Back To Glengarry' ... and the 'meringue white dress' photograph of the 16-year-old Glengarry debs was used in a magazine article. Leila wasn't a deb, and I was a reluctant one, but she identified the girls and updated me on who had died, which was a shock, and what the other 60-ish women were doing. My life had moved on, but hers was firmly in that geographic area. We had tea together and she said I looked exactly like my mother, of whom she was fond. Leila looked like her mother too.

So it was a shock to get an e-mail from an ex-schoolmate to

say that Leila had passed away in a nursing home and was to have a minimal graveside service. I decided to go but the burial was postponed to a time which was impossible for me to attend.

This was a generous-spirited woman who had been kind to others. I felt so guilty I had not kept in touch more. So this is my tribute to her. And she lives on in words which she hasn't read.

Westall's U.F.O.

U.F.O. is an unidentified flying object.

Westall High School's U.F.O. was a completely different kind of story. 1966 was my first year out teaching, and Westall, a raw, new suburb near Monash University, had many students from the migrant camp nearby. Most had limited English. I enjoyed my teaching there. One afternoon in April, many believe a U.F.O. was sighted. I have always said there was no U.F.O. but in subsequent interviews and documentaries, my comments always got lost.

Westall is now regarded internationally as an official U.F.O. sighting but I always said, 'It didn't happen.' Now there is a terrific kids' playground at The Grange, with a marker for the theme fantasy park with the story of the U.F.O. event ... A good outcome and my grandkids enjoyed the park.

Many of the former migrants are now skilled with their own families and leading productive lives and have a nostalgia for a common folktale.

And a blurred line between fiction and fact.

CHAPTER 18
BANNED, CONTROVERSIAL OR JUST DIFFICULT

Have you ever been banned?

I haven't been banned but a few of my books have been. Our *f2m: the boy within* was put on the banned shelf in a council library in outback Queensland the same week I was awarded an OAM for Literature at Government House in Melbourne. A few months before, *f2m: the boy within* was thrown in the bin at a literary festival by an English teacher, saying to her students, 'Don't read rubbish like that.' Guaranteed more readers immediately. And Kailash Studio made a documentary on reactions to this novel which has been screened at several festivals and is now on YouTube.

The 'smack' (not heroin) in *There's a Hippopotamus on Our Roof Eating Cake* provoked a weeklong media furor about child abuse when a new edition was released with suggested word changes by a new publisher of the 30-year-old classic. 'Growled' to replace the censored 'smack'. As everyone has been a child, and is an expert on childhood, 'smacking' or not, is a very emotive issue.

Occasionally fundamentalist schools object to content, like the steroids mentioned in *Gameplay*, one of the Frequent Flyer Twins series, but vital for the plot. I wasn't advocating use of sports drugs.

I don't have swearing, partly because it dates.

To discover your book is banned or a word condemned is a jolt, and makes you realise others do not read or think as you do.

Which books and why?

Often a story is rejected on subject matter, or condemned by non-readers. Fair enough if someone wishes to complain after they've read the book. But not if they haven't even opened the first page, or scrolled the initial screen.

f2m: the boy within, our 'coming of age' YA novel about Finn who transitions from female to male, was always likely to worry conservatives.

The subject of gender transition is controversial, not our compassionate handling of the character's situation with family and friends.

Picture book and later the app *Feymouse*, about a large and clumsy cat born into a family of highly talented mice, was condemned by a reviewer as a homosexual's 'coming out'. Not my intention at all. Coping successfully with being different is a common theme in my stories. And even if *Feymouse* were a 'gay' story, fine with me. But that wasn't my intention. Difficult when authors are condemned for interpretations of stories which they did not intend. But also revealing of reader prejudice.

Has your work ever been censored?

Sex, religion and politics are 'iffy' and likely to offend someone. But there's also a difference between writing 'propaganda' for a particular viewpoint, and exploring an issue or culture via a character's reaction.

Often a book is a 'safe' way of opening discussion on sensitive issues.

What is self-censorship?

Sometimes self-censorship of subject occurs by the author, aware that conservative readers will never see the book because apprehensive publishers are not willing to gamble financially on a 'controversial' subject.

Astute writers realise that satire or fantasy are techniques to enable discussion via symbolic characters set in another time or place, especially outer space. Animal or insect characters can often 'get away with' political, sexual or religious comment. Humour also helps. Propaganda or pushing one view only is a turn off.

I have avoided writing about indigenous characters because there are so many restrictions when you are not of a particular culture. But after researching Macedonian culture for *The Day My Friend Learnt to Dance*, complaints about my character not liking 'hot' chilli were taken as a cultural slur by the Macedonian hierarchy. So I concluded that an author should be androgynous and write about characters from genders other than own, and cultures other than those in which s/he was brought up, as long as the research was done well. Or my co-writer is culturally expert.

Q. Can You Discuss a Sample Project?

Our co-written *Hijabi Girl* project scored instant rejections from major publishers. 'Hijabi' in the title became a liability due to an escalation of anti-terrorist media coverage. The collaboration with a highly qualified Muslim children's librarian who wore a hijab wasn't enough. Fear of the unknown meant 'Islamic = terrorism' in some minds. 'Diversity' is fine in theory but in practice, sales matter.

Often the reasons for rejection are not the real ones. Professional authors accept frequent rejection because much depends upon timing, topicality, lists, curricula, and preferences of the publisher as well as quality of the writing. The most difficult project to place is where you are suggesting a new format for a subject they consider controversial or know little about. It takes a brave publisher to take the risk, and defend the proposal through monthly publishing meetings in big traditional houses. Frequently the smaller one-person publishers are more inclined to take the risk and often create the more innovative books.

Fiction is not autobiography but it can allow a reader the experience of living from the viewpoint of another, for the length of the book and beyond. And indirectly lead to more tolerance.

But the misconception that a Muslim character must be a terrorist needed to be challenged. As earlier in my *So Who's a Misfit?* stereotypes were challenged by the character of Crystal, as a non-Jewish student in a religious Jewish school. Even her name was symbolic. You can look through a crystal and see many facets.

For the *Hijabi Girl*, we favoured a picture book format so older students could use the visual clues in their learning of English. Fifteen rejections so far. And still counting.

Q. What has been the most difficult project to publish?

The ones you've never heard about.

CHAPTER 19
PARTICIPANT OBSERVATION

Experts & Naïve Readers

Participant observation is the excuse for adventures or 'stickybeaking'.

'I'm researching a book' has been my legitimate excuse for white-water rafting, doing the fire-safety course or flying on a big Sikorsky chopper to an oil rig with the engineer reluctantly holding my handbag. This excuse also covers eavesdropping, asking outrageous questions or barging slowly along French canals sipping local wine.

Great excuse or tax deductible? Both.

Some experience has been used in non fiction; other 'on site' happenings have helped create believable characters or settings. I spent a morning in a plumbing wholesalers to get the right details about pipes and toolkits for the picture book *Plato the Platypus Plumber, Part-time*. 98% of what I learnt I won't use in the story. But 2% is worth the visit, despite Plato's toolkit being used to fix grumpy people as well as plumbing emergencies. Another day scrambling around with the council engineer in waterways where urban platypus had been sighted. Gumboot research.

The difference between participant-observation and just 'doing adventurous stuff' is you visit with a purpose. You use all your senses. It may be the smell of lemon tea in the Nepali mountains after you've walked in the heat, or not being able to smell human waste in Antarctica. But you can smell pungent penguin poo! Sounds, sights, tastes and especially cheese soufflé on the gourmet French barge, and textures, all matter.

Greyhound ear tags mean you can't swap one dog for

another in a race, and this nearly messed up the plot of *Winning a Giraffe Called Geoffrey*. Lucky I checked that potential clue. A greyhound fan would know whether you knew what you were talking about. Or nearly mixing up long-line and net fishing can destroy or retain a reader's belief in the *Antarctic's Frozen Chosen* novel.

That's also why I use an 'expert' and a 'naïve' reader to check my manuscript. The 'naïve' reader is someone who just reads for the 'story' fun and is the target age or interest group. The 'expert' may be my original source scientist, customs officer or pilot or one who knows that area. This is my insurance that I've got it right. And sometimes I haven't.

In *Kendall, Mim and Temporary Fred* my under-age, unlicensed girl drives her almost-giving-birth mother to the maternity hospital and picks up a police–escort. I forgot to explain how she got the car home afterward without breaking the law again.

You 'participate' knowing that one of your characters might 'do' this later. Kyle, the Antarctic expeditioner, is the best example. I was scared of going over the side of the polar ship because you die in 4 minutes if you slip into icy Antarctic waters without the right gear. But I let him slip. I didn't. He did. But having been in the polar area, I had a more realistic idea of how he might feel about the awe-inspiring but dangerous ice.

To create a credible character, you need to get inside their world and understand procedures, skills and vocabulary that are new to you and to your reader.

If I hadn't gone to Antarctica, I wouldn't have experienced the translucent 'bergs, or how it feels when a chopper crashes on you. Or what a fool you feel if you mix up port and starboard for the lifeboat drill. I knew that 'port' was left because both have four letters … but which way was I supposed to be facing?

Another icy challenge was the *Titanic* Dog story. I found writing from the viewpoint of the sea dog to be a challenge. Plus the sad facts of the iceberg collision and the 'unsinkable' *Titanic* ship details and times had to be included. Historical details must be accurate.

Creating a character who is totally unlike the writer may be wish fulfillment or just skilled writing. But if you only ever write a version of yourself, you'll run out of material.

Viewpoints

I've been male. I've been a big cat. And I've even transitioned gender from female to male within the one novel. First person 'I' viewpoint is my preference to 'get inside' the character, who doesn't always have to be admirable. S/he can have nasty flaws. Or be arrogant. An easier viewpoint to sustain than 'nice'.

I 'go on location' to gather experience in a different setting, but the most valuable 'research' is not the geographic site but one or two phrases or an unexpected viewpoint which starts a plot I wasn't expecting.

Sometimes technology overtakes my clues. Now a 10-year-old would use a mobile or track via a digital device. So my stories either needed updating technologically or re-categorising the settings as period historic, like 1990s. With the new Sleuth Astrid chook, I invented a 'z-com' which wouldn't date.

Antarctic Writer on Ice

Antarctica was my most extreme research. And after we were beset in the polar ice for weeks and a chopper crashed, it was serious adventure. I'd applied to be a writer with the Australian Antarctic Division for the 'round-trip' resupply berth available for a non-scientist. I returned with facts and issues which fuelled many books, performances and talks. Yes, I became 'ice-affected' and look at icebergs and scientific issues with wonder and interest.

Jobs

At first you can draw on your own experience to give jobs and hobbies to your characters. Then you 'borrow' occupations of family and friends to get insider facts and funny stuff. In the Edwards family we have access to herbal gardening, infectious diseases, dog training, mapping, soccer, lingerie sales, belly-dancing, rehab, Rugby, Wagnerian opera, life-saving, cycling, Bridge card-playing, plumbing, jazz, community radio, markets, op shops, cooking and photo shoots.

Many writers cultivate a contact in each field. So they may have a quick source to check medical clues, or an expert on travel documents and I.D. Or poisons. Next comes in-depth 'day in the life of ...' interviews to get the viewpoints and routines right. Mechanics. Tree-loppers. Market-stall holders. Potters.

Writers need to be active listeners.

Occasionally extra training is needed. Some crime and mystery writers have done short courses in debt-collecting, pathology or private investigator training to get authentic details for their books. Even criminology.

I've done fire-safety training and search & rescue plus behind-the-scenes in a funeral parlour and Emergency wards. I've also been taken to the early morning flower markets, by a local who explained what was really going on amongst the local Mafia. I've travelled in police cars. I've done a massage course.

Belly dancing has been my 'play' even though I'm still in class 101 after more than a decade. I love wafting the veil around and learning from my Monday night classmates who lead completely different lives. Initially I was asked by a TV channel to write a script for their Bookworm puppet character for a special Olympic Games program. Deciding that maybe he could belly dance, I rang up a few classes. One was upset by my motivation and suggested I was trivialising Middle Eastern art. Another welcomed me and I was seduced by the music. But realised my mistake. The worm had no arms and couldn't hold up a veil to dance. So I scripted him a hula hoop for the children's TV program and continued with the belly-dancing myself, for fun. Later I used the experience for my belly-dancing pig and to start a class in Antarctica for female expeditioners beset in the polar ice. That was a first. We used ship's towels, as veils are not usually available in a Viking polar expedition ship. Exercise to music, but it made the Sky news. An unusual anti-boredom strategy.

The job of marriage celebrant is a possible sleuth character. She could move around various cultures and conflict scenes. Versatile enough for several plots. Not sure about studying the course yet.

Authors are often asked, 'What would you do if you weren't a writer?' Usually I say, 'I'd run an ice-cream parlour.'

CHAPTER 20
TREKKING IN NEPAL

New Woman, a glossy magazine, published my double-page 'Trekking in Nepal' feature with photos. Ironically I was meeting a friend for a coffee in South Melbourne, and noticed the magazine in the café, open: the previous coffee drinker, who was a stranger, had been reading that article and looking at my photos.

An unexpected thrill for me and I gave into temptation. When I left the café, I arranged the magazine open at that page. Authors (and their trained family members) tend to turn face out the covers of their books in bookshops. Booksellers can always tell which authors have visited and don't mind, as long as authors buy other books.

Nepal was a working assignment, not just a holiday. Articles went into various anthologies and magazines. The angle was women leaders facing physical challenges at a point of change in their lives.

Spirited Women

Why would eighteen women, aged 45–55, from veteran mountaineers to those of 'very average' fitness, go trekking in Nepal as a Spirited Women's group?

Like childbirth, trekking upwards is relentless. Zigzagging slowly. Getting to know intimately the shape of the next trekker's boots. Occasionally looking up at the peaks. Afterwards, you remember only the exhilaration of completing it, and not the mid response: 'I must never let myself get into this situation again.'

I felt morally obliged to go, partly because the spirited women's concept had grown out of my witty women's lunch. Guests brought food, linked to a quote by or about a witty woman. 'Spirited Adventure' had been the theme for last year's meal, held in the former church in Gembrook now owned by psychologist-trekker Judy Parker.

'Why not hold the next witty dinner in Nepal?' was the suggestion.

So we ended up in Kopah Gompa, a Tibetan Buddhist monastery in Kathmandu. The High Lama blessed the trekkers after a ten-minute meditation. Difficult for Western aching knees not to turn the soles towards the lama, signifying disrespect.

The trekkers' occupations ranged from the hydroponics tomato-grower and ex-pilot, hobby farmers and nurses to a principal and her student daughter. A psychologist, a social worker, and a hospital scientist who had climbed Mt Kilimanjaro made up the group. Four sisters had paddled the Murray marathon canoe race. They were the fit ones.

Planned was six days trekking, followed by white-water rafting to the Royal Chitwan Wildlife National Park. The real aim was a meditative journey of the spirit for invited women at a point of reflection. Entering the post-family responsibilities phase, some had time for self, ideas or philosophical exploration.

How did the women cope?

'A memorable experience. I'd go again tomorrow.'

'I coped better than expected, except for the leeches.'

'The peaks are breath-taking, literally.'

I'd say that it was hard physically, but the company was terrific. Flying beside the Himalayas was postcard stuff. The culture shock of Kathmandu Airport came with beggars, holy men and touts. Resourceful Nima Lama, our multi-lingual guide, sorted out trekking visas, passports, baggage and currencies.

Two nights in Kathmandu before flying to Pokhara to begin the trek. My apprehension about fitness persisted.

Our apprentice trek began the next afternoon with thousands of steps leading up to the Swambunath temple. Judy led us through Kathmandu back streets, past rubbish, wandering sacred cows, smiling sellers and even a dead dog on a rubbish heap. Streets with hovels, coughing and spitting, open meat stalls and yet smiling, courteous locals. Several of our group turned vegetarian immediately.

'Don't allow the dogs or monkeys to touch you,' warned Judy. 'Rabies.'

Swambunath Temple was festooned with monkeys, slinking dogs, beggars and even a snake charmer. My training climbs on the thousand steps in Melbourne's Sherbrooke Forest were kindergarten stuff!

An all-female trekking group led by an Australian Buddhist woman who could speak some Nepali was unusual. Not only were we very old, in a country where life expectancy is 50, but the support crew of sirdah (organiser), 7 sherpas, 7 cooks and 27 porters were male.

We were warned about the leg-injured 'large American lady with the boobs' carried out over two days by four sherpas in twenty minute rotations. Since Nepalis balance heavy loads by holding headbands, this was impossible with a lady who draped over their shoulders.

I was determined not to become a mountain anecdote, however respectfully told.

Only boiled water was safe. Supplies were short. Rather than wash our own clothes, we were asked to pay locals, enabling them to earn money. Tasks we felt we were physically capable of doing. This worried us.

Meanwhile, a brilliant flight with mountain views. In Pokhara airport, eager porters left for our first mountain camp, after lashing our bags on their backs. Determinedly carrying daypacks, we followed up into the mountains. About 1.30 p.m. our cooks, whom we didn't yet recognise, came running back with a kettle of lemon tea and tin mugs. A memorable drink. We waded through rivers, walked across a swing bridge and looked up to see a picnic lunch laid out with a view. A rest. Legs like jelly.

Another couple of hours walking on river flats, and then arriving to witness our purple Himalayan tents already erected.

'We made it,' was the general response.

Bathing discreetly in the river was a bonus, not fully appreciated until days later. Water became limited to a morning bowl and your bottle.

'M'am.' Overnight, the sherpa guard shone the torch towards the toilet tent known as 'The palace'. The ability to squat was becoming a necessary skill. What you looked like didn't matter. Whether your body worked, did.

Meanwhile, I'd nappy-pinned a towel around me for respectability. My Sam's pants (bought in Kathmandu) split further at each upward step. Mid-afternoon, only the waist band and lower legs were left. Our other clothes had vanished mountainwards on the porters' backs. After an early 10.30 a.m. lunch, determined by the availability of water, we trekked upwards. Most days we started trekking about 7.30 a.m. with an hour lunch break, in order to arrive before 4.30 p.m. when the rains came down.

Women with Altitude

2 p.m. 34 degrees.

I was finding it hard to breathe. And I was unexpectedly 'flooding', something I later discovered happened to other women at altitude. Even harder was admitting that I needed help. Other women shared their resources. Giving me her stick, Judy gave my backpack to a sherpa. Then she told me to follow exactly in her slow zig-zag steps.

'Stop thinking. Just follow. It saves 50% of your energy. If you're panting, you're going too fast, it puts too much strain on your heart.'

So I went into slow motion. I looked only at Judy's boots. I stopped worrying about the sherpa carrying my load. I knew that if I didn't have help, I wouldn't make it. A regular swimmer, I had not expected to have trouble breathing, despite the altitude. I lost sense of time. I just climbed.

For independent women, accepting help is a significant experience. Later Judy stressed, 'There's a difference between "dependence" and "inter-dependence". You help each other, when it's necessary.'

Climbing cautiously downhill, it was okay to do the Nepali waltz, which meant accepting a sherpa's hand ... And as everybody's Sam-bought pants split, others would lend pins or scarves.

Leeches were a constant problem.

'Spray Rid on your bare feet, then your socks, then your shoes.'

Porters carried food, bedding and cookingware in open weave baskets called dokos. Some wore plastic bags on their thonged feet to deter the leeches. Obsessional checking for leeches with torches interrupted dinner in the meal tent.

'Leeches can live for two years without a meal,' explained Judy.

Our own dinner had three courses of soup, rice or potatoes, meat and tinned fruit. Judy presented each woman with a leaf from Buddha's tree. 'Represents enlightenment.'

How Far Did You Go?

Appreciating the Nepali generosity of spirit, we wanted to help without appearing condescending. Many are illiterate and books are prized. Judy had asked us to carry in donated books for an orphanage. Our 'spirited' women have since arranged ongoing educational support.

'How far did you go in Nepal?

Did you mean the seventy kilometres we trekked, the 10,000 feet we climbed or the 100 kilometres rafted? Or did you mean the personal journey?'

As a writer I was fascinated by how a group of women who were usually leaders managed to help each other in challenging physical circumstances. Without the experience of writing about adventurous Nepal, I would never have gone on an Antarctic expedition as writer.

CHAPTER 21
ANTARCTIC WRITER ON ICE

Fake Adventurer

As an Antarctic adventurer, I felt a fake. I don't even like the cold. Antarctica was not a lifelong passion as it was for many. Antarctica was up there with the Himalayas and climbing Everest. Mt Everest was never on my 'to-do' list either, although I trekked in Nepal beneath the Himalayan mountains which I pronounce Him-A-Lay-An, not Hi-MARL-I-An as is now fashionable.

Words like 'trekking' and 'expeditioner' sound so adventurous, but across the years I found myself in risky situations and places which others considered 'adventurous' only because I was intrigued by why they went there or did that. Observing others' risky passions made me a kind of literary voyeur, but unless I became a participant–observer, I couldn't write accurately about what they felt and did, even if it were very different from my personal inclinations.

'Why don't you apply for the Antarctic berth as writer?'

'Are you a gambler? No? Want to write about the pokies obsession?'

'How about coming to China and walking the Great Wall?'

When seduced by an invitation to a risky challenge by an energetic host, I tend to say yes and then work out how I'll cope. Willpower is not always enough when the challenge is physical. That's why I was nervous about Antarctic physical challenges, because I'd been affected by altitude in Nepal. So I knew that it was possible that my body might not be able to do what my brain dictated. Often I have doubts beforehand, but when I'm there, it's too late.

And the gap between aspiration, reality and failure is real

writing.

Antarctica was definitely the biggest risk and the greatest adventure.

How did I find myself in the ice?

A couple of years earlier, I'd heard there was an Australian Antarctic Division berth for a non-scientist. This is now called an Antarctic Arts Fellowship. Children's author–illustrator Coral Tulloch had been 'Down South', as it's called, for a summer, and when I saw her iceberg illustrations I fell in love with the 'bergs'. They weren't just white. They had tinges of pink, blue and jade from the overturned plant life. Jade bergs seduced me.

I didn't expect to get the berth but decided to apply for the round-trip resupply voyage and take up reading about Antarctica as a hobby. There are winterers, the elite who stay all year, summerers who work summer months November to March, and the lowly roundtrippers who are part of the working crew for the annual resupply of food and fuel and the 'changeover' of staff of each base. 'Roundtripper' voyages are shorter, at about three weeks' voyage each way to Mawson, plus five days to 'changeover crew and supplies' as the longest, unless you become beset in the polar ice or weather conditions deteriorate. I was more interested in a voyage to Casey Station, which was closer and therefore shorter. In theory.

Competition for the 'berth' was intense, plus stringent physical and psychological tests. You had to propose a project which needed to be researched in Antarctica but which could be published internationally. When I first applied for the humanities berth, I didn't anticipate a chopper crash, becoming beset in the polar ice with 34 blokes, nor Garnet getting a next-of-kin call. I was fairly sure I'd get enough material about Antarctic workstyles on the bases to write something but was relying on serendipitous extras. I got them. And ended up writing more about Antarctica in varied formats for different age groups than any other subject. I became ice-affected, as it's called. Antarctica changes everyone.

I fell in love with the icebergs as symbols: like book writing, nine-tenths is out of sight and only 10% visible. Plus in that surreal icescape, I was aware that only words could capture emotions and experiences to overcome a sense of human insignificance in that vast icescape.

Although mentally adventurous and willing to take a risk with ideas, my physical adventure gene was weak. 'Adventure' or finding myself in extreme physical challenges was cumulative for me. Often I said 'yes' to a writing opportunity and then found myself in a challenging situation where there was no choice. It wasn't courage; it was just having no further options.

Orienteering gave me basic camping and map-reading skills. If I hadn't orienteered reluctantly on Sundays for years, and got lost regularly, I wouldn't have considered walking the 4 days of the Milford Track in New Zealand to celebrate my 50th birthday and plot a mystery en route. The remoteness of Antarctica hit me later, on the voyage, when the Norwegian ice pilot on the bridge of the *Polar Bird* confirmed that some of the polar ice ahead of us had never been mapped.

Then the word 'Expeditioner' is terrifying.

Words are a way of coming to terms with the 'surreal' nature of Antarctica, once you've run out of film. And you have time to think. 'Wintering' or being ice-bound provides that time.

Pre-expedition, fear got me the fittest I'd ever been. Aged 55 and my definition of fit wasn't near the ex-marathoner males on board. 55 is the cut-off age for first-time working expeditioners. So friends 'walked' me, escorting me up and down the steps when my will power waned. I'd learnt from my Milford Track experience, you need to practise not just walking longer distances but stepping up ... and get your calf muscles acquainted with down ... which is actually harder.

Reading about historic Antarctica and the Australian bases of Casey, Mawson and Davis became my hobby. Authors need three hobbies to go on the back cover with their bio, so I decided to add 'reading about Antarctica'. If I didn't get chosen for the round trip or pass the medical, I could at least have a hobby for my book blurbs.

They sent me the male medical checklist by mistake. I don't have a prostate. But they then sent the female medical checklist. So I had no excuse.

Originally I asked my family if I should apply.

'Great idea for you to go to the ends of the earth,' teased Garnet.

'I'll look after the e-mails.' Kim offered me thick socks and snowballs.

Trevelyan said, 'Go for it Mum.'

Son-in-law Dave didn't think I'd pass the medical, which is comparable to that for pilots. Neither did I, but that would give me another respectable and acceptable excuse to drop out.

In Melbourne, after a day of strenuous testing, they gave me the medical I.D. card with my blood group and Antarctic Expeditioner as occupation. I was thrilled momentarily.

My Antarctic geography was hazy. But I had nine months and started with geographic features named after women. Not many. Only royal sponsors or lovers, like the Adelie penguin named after the wife of the French explorer Captain Dumont d'Urville. Just seven women had been station leaders on Australian bases. I started reading about them.

But most Antarctic books and photos were about hairy males with icy beards and heroic aspirations. History wasn't about who was physically strong enough to walk on ice, but who was politically adept to get the permissions and support to do so.

Leaders needed to be able to raise the money and equip their trip, have charm to keep sponsors happy, and be respected by their peers. And timing and mystique mattered. The public likes heroes.

I admired their single-mindedness, but questioned what actually made a good leader and an explorer. And whether sheer physical risk-taking was the only form of courage. And what was the fine line between stubborn stupidity and bravery. Was there an adventure gene, and if so, was it dominant or recessive, like mine?

What interested me most was the motivations of the expeditioners and trekkers. Were they running to adventure or away from home and domesticity? And was the power structure amongst these highly able people based on physical fitness, professional skills or other qualities? What happens in an extreme and isolated setting like Antarctica when a woman was the appointed station leader of males?

Nepalese mountaineering had similar challenges. Were the spirited women leaders likely to compete for leadership roles on a Nepalese trek where each fit female was used to being in charge? I was second bottom of the Nepali Trek fitness stakes, below the marathon runners, canoeists and athletes, and had no aspirations to leadership. I just wanted to keep up, and was scared I wouldn't make my quota of kilometres each day, especially upwards. Likewise on the Antarctic ice, I was concerned I wouldn't be able to climb fast enough in and out of vehicles like Haggs and vessels like barges.

Beset: Hazel on the *Polar Bird*

I've always used the excuse of *writer* to explain my presence in adventurous places despite my lack of intense training prior to the event. If you've done it and observed others struggling, you add the technical terms and local knowledge and languages that make the experience real for the reader. Plus you need to be candid about your fears and stuff-ups. So if you make no claim to being a well-prepared and super-fit adventurer, there isn't so much embarrassment in admitting worry about bush toilets, crevasse-falling or being seasick or altitude-affected. Being unable to get dressed in emergency gear in the time limit and into the correct lifeboat is another challenge, excused by being the writer.

As part of a working expedition, not a cruise ship, and in the role of writer, I was unsure what other skills I had to swap in a cashless society of highly able male problem-solvers who were also Boffins and Tradies. Later I swapped writing e-mail love letters for the barge-master to send his girlfriend, on the understanding that he'd get my backside in the barge when I went over the side of the ship. Our literary exchange worked. Words are part of the exchange rate.

The Lachie-berg

Six-year-old neighbour Lachie had requested that I write an Antarctic story using his name. Seduced by translucent iceberg beauty, and because the guys had jokingly named one 'Hazelberg' I wrote a story about a jade iceberg. I checked the facts with the glaciologist onboard and e-mailed it to Lachlan. Then the requests started. Expeditioners with young families wanted a copy to e-mail with their child's name on. E-mails are vital communication with Antarctic families and it's important to have news other than 'we're still stuck at such and such degrees.' So I put a male and a female version of the 'iceberg' story on the communal e-mail computer for downloading.

Since I was researching my eco-thriller, being ice-bound

with Antarctic experts on law, illegal long-line fishing, Patagonian Tooth-fish, ele-seals, polar pilots, diesos and electronic 'Gods' who fixed satellite links for e-mail was actually a benefit. Bored, they were delighted to help me plot. Skills swap.

My Antarctic journey was a state of mind as much as an expedition to Casey Station. I expected the major challenge to be coping with the cold or the crevasse field training. Instead, it was the imaginative challenge of using words to come to terms with the scope of Antarctica. And trying to use the F.U.D. (female urinary device) while wearing thermals, ventiles (wind proofs), balaclavas, woollen jackets, boots with chains and the polar immersion survival suit.

Camaraderie exists between most ex-Antarctic expeditioners. They keep in touch. And I'm flattered they include me, and value my Antarctic books, whereas I was a bit concerned they might think I was intruding.

Midwinter Dinner
Casey Station
Wilkes Land
Antarctica

Mr & Mrs Hazel Edwards (embarrassed they couldn't remember Garnet's name)

> The men of the 54th ANARE cordially request the pleasure of your company at Midwinter Dinner, on Thursday the 21st June, 2001
>
> Pre-dinner drinks at two o'clock in the afternoon
>
> Dinner at three o'clock
>
> Formal dress and decorations
>
> Transportation may be provided by arrangement from the ice edge, somewhere north of 66° South, 110° East in the Southern Ocean
>
> Carriages at ten o'clock

R.S.V.P.

Subject: RSVP for Midwinter Dinner

Dear Men of 54th ANARE

I'd be delighted to accept your invitation to the Midwinter Dinner at Casey Station in Wilkes Land Antarctica on Thursday 21st June. It is the longest night here, but I guess yours will be longer but I have a slight transport problem. Walking (or shanks pony) was one option, but it will take years, and I don't like to be late for functions.

Skiing was one possibility but the Great Southern Ocean is fairly challenging in an up-and-down kind of way.

Parachuting was another possibility, but the chute might freeze mid-air, and roof-crashing into the Red Shed seemed a little like gate-crashing the party.

The carriage from the ice-edge sounded enticing, but I have

to get there first.

My tri-weekly swimming tends to be 20 laps, not 2000 nautical miles …

So unless you can arrange a fly-over to an airfield iceberg near you, I'll have to decline your invitation.

But I'll be there in spirit.

Hazel

Hot Ice-Squad

Mistakenly I'd assumed it would be easy to create a cast of Antarctic vehicles, with personalities, set on 'Windmill', a hypothetical Australian Base in remote Antarctica.

I started with the idea of a 'Six Pack' of ice vehicles because 'vehicle' was too difficult to read for the target age of 3–8-year-olds, and strictly speaking the Zodiac, which was an inflatable rubber duck, was not a vehicle. Neither were the helicopters which sling-loaded supplies.

Against the ice, the vivid primary colours were practical, because expeditioners could find their transport and colour-coded huts, like the Red Shed or the Green Store, in blizzard conditions.

Naming Characters:

My first decision was to name the characters by their roles or brands because I had a cast of humans and vehicles.

Antarctic vehicles are known by their brand names, like Hagg which is short for the Swedish tracked Hagglund, or Quad for the four wheeled motor cycle. That provided the names, as did the expeditioners' roles like Dieso (mechanic), Chippie (carpenter), Doc, Met Guy (meteorologist) or Birdo who was a scientist studying birds. Expeditioners are either 'boffins' (scientists who include astro-physicists, glaciologists and environmental impact specialists) or 'tradies' support staff including the chef, plumber or Comm God who is the electrical communications expert. Under-eights find those job titles hard to read. Luckily,

Antarctica is the land of abbreviations like 'birdo' or 'bio' and nicknames like Critter, but naming my characters was still a challenge. I decided to link an expeditioner with each vehicle and make either the Dieso or the S.L. (Station Leader) the major human character for continuity.

Technical decisions had to be made. Could a vehicle actually talk on the radio? Or use a G.P.S. (global positioning system)? Could a Hagg get seasick? Did the 'Hot Ice Pack' speak to their expeditioners? Or vice versa? What was the relationship between the vehicle and its main driver? Was the vehicle equal or dominant?

I used colour, numbers and attributes like 'slow and steady' for the Hagg, while the Quad was an adolescent who 'hooned' around. Gender was another issue. The 'Copter Twins became female and so did the Zodiac, whom I called Zip as she disliked being known as 'Rubber Duckie'.

As they 'winter' on the ice, the Dieso keeps them moving while they cope with fire alarms, search-and-rescue (SAR) and even blizzards.

'The A Factor' is what it's called when things go wrong in Antarctica, so I wanted the theme of working together and effective problem-solving. Helicopters do travel in pairs for safety in Antarctica, so the 'Copter Twins were born as impulsive larrikins, while Mr. Muscles became the 'grunt' who provide shelter during a blizzard for the lighter vehicles who were in danger of being blown away.

An Australian Antarctic Base is a mixture of hi-tech via satellite, and resourceful 'fixing' when things don't work in the cold.

On Base, there is a web-cam which photographs station-life and sends it back via Internet for families and colleagues. I decided to use the web-cam as a device to provide flashback, multi-media links and a way of characterising egos.

Eventually, I hope that one day my 'Antarctic Hot Ice Pack' will challenge Thomas the Tank Engine in various storytelling mediums.

Fan-tartic

After my return I was interviewed a lot as a female expeditioner my age was a novelty.

Q. You experienced an on-board helicopter crash and were beset in the ice for eighteen days. What life skills did you learn?

A. I learnt from the other expeditioners how to respond fast in dangerous situations like possible polar fire, but also how to cope with long stretches of enforced inactivity due to blizz conditions. I learnt the value of words and creativity in coming to terms with the significance of extreme situations and the sheer size of Antarctica and your own insignificance—having an imagination helps a lot! A sense of humour needs to be tested on the medical!

A sense of humour and creativity are survival skills greater than any form of physical strength.

Q: What would you say is the single most important thing you learnt in Antarctica and can apply in your writing?

A. An appreciation of the natural world including weather, icebergs and marine life and your personal insignificance. An Antarctic literary tradition is beginning and it's exciting to think there is a new literary genre. I've become a Fan-tarctic, a fan of Antarctica.

Now there's a group of Australian female Antarctic expedition authors who call themselves the 'Orange Roughies'. Co-incidentally, all have red hair. Mine is dyed, but author-expeditioner Jesse Blackadder's red hair is real.

CHAPTER 22
IDEAS ADDICT: WHY DO YOU WRITE?

Primarily I write to avoid or alleviate the boredom of routine. And to have a legitimate reason for being 'nosy' when I'm just plain curious about others' lives and like to ask intrusive questions. And gather ideas. Typically, I ask:
What was your biggest challenge?
What gave the greatest satisfaction?
Tell me about a typical day at your work? What really annoys you? What could go wrong around here?

Fiction gives me a reason to closely observe my surroundings and listen with a purpose to talkative people or even 'bores'. No-one is really boring, you just have to find their interests by asking the right questions. Non-fiction gives me an excuse to interview passionate people about their jobs, hobbies or lives, secret and mundane.. And once I've got the rough structure of the story, I start enjoying the process, especially the quirky viewpoints or motives.

The ways of writing might be routine, although I do experiment with new media, but the subject changes. And so do the age and interest groups.

Colleagues influence me. Often I collaborate on projects and indirectly learn from others' passion. Or I learn technical hints like how to record using new devices, but still it is the quality of the human story which matters most.

I became interested in gaming and pokies addiction and only later realised the similarity of the risk factor in 'punting' on an idea for a story in a difficult publishing market. The odds are slightly better than the pokies, but not much. Addiction was a topic I had to research for a health project and discovered I fitted the criteria. I was an ideas addict.

Where Do You Get Time to Write?

By not doing other things. Changing priorities. I don't iron and rarely shop.

I'm conscious that my stamina fades mid-afternoon now, and whereas I could put in bursts of 10-hour writing days, I can't do that any more. I work best for 3–4 hours early in the day and then I fade. So if I am to finish this memoir, I have to give it priority. Also a way of ensuring I tidy up legal literary papers.

If you don't record in some way, it's lost!

Knowing that I may write about something afterwards has kept me interested at weddings, airports and picking up my children after school, at sport, nightclubs or after work. Writing has enabled me to keep ennui at bay, but not all the time. So I'm grateful for being an author.

'If you'd inherited money, would you still have been an author?'

Yes. But maybe I would have bought the channel of distribution of the ideas?

CHAPTER 23
WHY COLLABORATE?

Co means Together

Collaborating with an author or illustrator is a bit like marriage. Some relationships work and some end in separation or divorce. This is not the time to Kiss and Tell about what worked less successfully than expected, because the praise or blame should be shared.

Most of my collaborations have been fun, and productive. Problems arise when the projects don't get up or marketing circumstances change. Ironically, it's the financially successful ideas which cause the most angst. Often the collaborators can't remember who did what and when. And by the end of a project, they've often learnt the others' skills, and no longer defer.

The best collaborations are when different skills are brought together and equally respected. While collaborators may not spend equal time, the quality of contribution needs to be equal. One may have expert knowledge or experience but the other has more crafting skills to convey that. As I get older, I've found myself working with younger collaborators because they have the physical or technical skills I lack. And they're enthusiastic and energetic. That's why I've recently taken on an intern.

Writing tends to be a solitary occupation, so having a regular meeting time overcomes procrastination and ensures your share is ready for the next meeting. More sociable too. Often writing partners become friends. Co-scriptwriting is the most fun, especially if you act out roles. I loved being a grumpy, belly-dancing male pig in *Duckstar*. And I learnt about pacing on stage from co-writer Christine, who is also a theatre director, plus we listened to relevant upbeat music while we wrote.

Never forget racing to our local library to get the Grand March from *Aida* to play as background for our satire of a duck with director attitude. These days we'd download instantly. I only like classical music with OOOMPH and *Aida* has that. Allocating roles to read aloud differentiates and deepens characterisation. That male, grumpy belly-dancing pig could dance.

A few creators are vague about the financial and rights details, and this can limit future adaptations into new media as rights become complicated, and good work has to be abandoned for legal reasons. Frustrating when you know you were the originator of the concept but have to spend ages finding the piece of paper which proves that. When illustrated stories move into new media, proposals get very complicated because the rights to illustrations often require permissions involving intellectual property lawyers who earn more per minute than the originators get for the project.

Collaborating with family members is even more challenging. I've observed a few mismatches of skills and time for those writing family histories. However, writing *Cycling Solo: Ireland to Istanbul* with son Trevelyan was an acknowledged split of skills. I did the business and he cycled and wrote the draft manuscript which I finished. And we're still talking to each other.

Another kind of collaboration has been writing grandkids' birthday stories like *Henry-Garnet, the Serial Sock Puller*, based on photos but also events significant to them that year. That's been fun and a project I've shared with other grandparents.

Unexpected Benefits

I've learnt something different from each collaborator. Via *f2m: the boy within*, Ryan taught me how to plot on Skype, updated me electronically with book trailers, a New Zealand–Melbourne book launch on webcam and a YouTube doco about reactions to our subject. With each collaborator I've learnt about another world; but the gender diverse world of transitioning had a new vocabulary, and appropriate pronouns were vital. You don't wish to inadvertently insult or hurt by saying 'she' instead of 'he' or vice versa. I also learnt to admire the courage of those forced to live differently because of their gender.

Psychologist Helen McGrath taught me new vocabulary for emotions I already knew, but I learnt to recognise sociopaths and that carried over into the creation of my fictional characters, especially for crime or thrillers. Ironically we lost our chapter on Anxiety in cyberspace, and that caused some anxiety for both co-authors.

Goldie Alexander and I wrote educational series and scripts in areas which we were teaching. We read aloud and laughed. Goldie formatted for us, as I was hopeless at that.

People often ask how collaboration works. Do we sit at the same desk? Who is the ideas person? Generally what works is a combination of e-mail, tracking edits, Skype conversations and meeting face-to-face, often in cafes. This is known as The Cappuccino Approach with the odd embarrassing moment where eavesdropping coffee drinkers have assumed our dialogue was a real conversation, rather than us acting out a crime scene.

Digital innovations have made co-writing easier. In the beginning, the early morning writer fowl would work on the current draft until brain-dead 2–3 hours later. Then the story draft would be e-mailed to the night writer 'owl'. Until the next draft was e-mailed back, no further work was to be done. 'Over to you' was the message. This provided a thinking break, but also a moral obligation to work when it did arrive. Today, we share a file online, instantly.

Co-writing fiction is harder than factual writing where chapters are often based on answers to the most common 'How To …' questions. But a co-writer who is a built-in editor is a bonus.

Multi-Media Myths

The greatest time-wasters can be gambling on big multi-media projects, which involve elaborate proposals and sample, expensive prototypes, with a multiplicity of collaborators. Then the projects don't happen because the funding fell through. Animation, film and TV series fit in this category. Often later there can be legal complications about who owns what from the discarded projects, which just might be recycled in a new myth.

The positive side is that you meet some fascinating artists in allied fields. And occasionally it gives you skills for your next project. I get seduced every time, not by the million dollar mythical carrots but by the enthusiasm and energy of promoters.

CHAPTER 24
CHARITABLE OVERLOAD

Social Issues

I've been attracted to issues like fostering, adoption, genetic counselling, fire-safety, medical research, therapy pets like Honey the Hospital Dog, grief and loss counselling and funeral parlours, child accidents, police, graffiti, racial and gender prejudice, pokies addiction, asylum seekers and bullying. Plus ice-cream making.

Inevitably authors are attracted to social, ecological or political issues and tend to write in fact or fiction about the impact of those conflicts on their characters. Writing easily-read, illustrated fiction about an individual character's problem can portray a wider issue, and attract support in a different way than cash donations. A poignant story is more memorable than statistics.

'Ambassador' in the literary world means elastic donations of time and autographed books for a specific charity. 'Reading Ambassador' is a title bestowed by many organisations associated with literacy and children. And when it is prefixed with 'National', and put on a business card, e- or name-tag, it looks impressive.

Accepting the title of Ambassador is inappropriate unless you are genuinely working for that cause at your own cost.

All authors face this charitable dilemma of 'How much?' One solution is to privately support my chosen charities but on my terms. If the expectation of the host's invitation is that I'll give my services, that is different from my choosing to do so.

I donate my time in fund-raising talks, but unless I have a private personal interest in that illness or a child from my family or friends is involved, I'm not prepared to donate my writing time to create a book which is sold on behalf of the organisation. Indigenous children or asylum seekers are overwhelmingly hard to refuse as a group, so I help individuals who make things happen rather than multi-level, multi-national charities.

Compassion Overload occurs for some authors over-exposed to highly paid corporate individuals who gain status or tax deductions from the worthy project or professionals paid for their contributions, while authors are expected to donate their time and autographed books at their own cost. This is the hidden aspect about which few authors comment in public.

Just in Case You Visit the Children's Court

Illustrator Michael Salmon and I were involved by Legal Aid and the Children's Court to create an easy-to-read, accessible book which explained the court processes, for parents and kids. Lots of research of heartbreaking cases, but this guided the format of illustrations and the use of appropriate humour in structuring the book in comic style. This book became a best-*giver* rather than a bestseller as the court issued it to child and parent clients, as even those adults with literacy problems could use it.

Writing by committee is always a challenge, especially when most are lawyers who want top billing. But when the subject genuinely makes a difference, there is quiet satisfaction.

Real Literacy Ambassadors

As I get older I prefer to support the work of enthusiastic and genuine individuals, often without titles, who make a difference.

A pattern emerges. An innovator has a good idea and that altruistic passion attracts supporters and donated resources. But then it becomes formalised, and the original supporters get so frustrated with red tape and how donations are used that they go elsewhere.

I've decided to stick with helping the individuals. Especially in Asia, people like educator Aileen Hall have been long-term advocates for Australian children's books and literacy. Gallery owner and illustrator Ann James has toured exhibitions sharing the work of quality illustrators and authors. Educator Maureen Ryan has featured the artwork of refugee children.

Although not a committee person, I try to give back to peers via being on the board of the Australian Society of Authors. That's practical.

Awards

'Award-winning' is the ubiquitous phrase on the back cover of many books.

It's customary for authors to say that reader response matters more than awards. But that's not entirely true. Responses from fans are precious. However, significant awards increase the chances of your book getting into the minds of more readers.

And as often an author is a solo worker, it helps to have an organisation supporting publicity and administration. Then potential readers can judge the book because they have access to it. They can't read something they've never heard of or can't buy because there's no distribution locally.

Which awards do I value most?
The ones where nominated by peers.

Being nominated three times for the international Astrid Lindgren Memorial Award is a matter of personal pride because the nomination is for a body of work, in the spirit of the feisty Swedish female author Astrid, and only a few from each country are included. Equally delighted when Australian Shaun Tan won it in 2011, as this draws attention to the work of all children's authors and illustrators.

That's why I'm also grateful to my colleagues who nominated me for the Order of Australia Medal (O.A.M.) for Literature in the 2013 Queens Birthday Honours and for the Australian Society of Authors (A.S.A.) Medal in 2009. This is a beautiful 'storytelling' themed pendant crafted by an indigenous artist.

At first I felt a little embarrassed at wearing my O.A.M. pin on formal jackets, but my husband insisted that was the protocol. I'd never noticed others' badges and the significance of medals before. The Government House ceremony was a wonderful celebration, brilliantly organised, and I felt great pride at crossing the red carpet to meet the Governor in the alphabetical vicinity of cyclist Cadel Evans, as we were both E.

Friends joked that the cake eating hippo, not me, got an O.A.M. for Outsized Awesome Myth.

O.A.M. was added to my e-tag and letterhead, and I do wear my medal for literary events. But it also draws attention to the whole artistic creator community and the cultural significance of authors.

O.A.M. award at Government House 2013

CHAPTER 25
'MEMORABLE' AUTHOR VISIT

Memorable?

Early starts, island-hops on planes and adapting to time zones are the norm for author tours. I wear flat shoes, drip-dry clothing in a single colour, plus scarf layers so I can add or take off according to fast weather changes.

Being a minimalist author on tour who washes her one set of clothes overnight gave me one of my most embarrassing moments.

My hosts put me up in a recently renovated bedroom, on the second floor within the writers' centre with a separate bathroom down the long passageway, where I hung my entire drip-dry set of clothes, including underwear. Unaware of anyone staying after midnight, burglars broke into the ground floor offices. My choices were to confront them naked, with the doona around me, creep down to retrieve my damp clothes first or retire to bed. Luckily the police arrived immediately. And now I never wash 'everything' overnight. Always keep one dry wrap-around top in case of burglar emergencies.

'Memorable' is the ambiguous comment I use when asked about an event which was really bad or most enjoyable.

Having a pizza delivered to the nearest palm tree, while sunset-watching with Darwin librarians, was memorable in the best way.

Generous locals escort you around their workplace or share scenic spots like crocodile-infested waters, heritage buildings like Fremantle Maximum Security Jail or even the explosions of Kempsey fireworks farm where colour recipes exist for fireworks, rather like cooking.

Fascinating to discover that the booming pyrotechnics business in a recycled farm employed mainly middle-aged women.

'We drive slower and don't set off the fireworks like hooning young blokes.'

One bonus is that those locations and facts are often used in later stories. 'Ordinary' is exotic to visitors, especially writers.

Parents are grateful for role-models of creative self-employment, book ideas and help with literacy. 'Kids only know about what jobs their parents do.'

And sharing local myths and tall stories which are sometimes hard to distinguish from 'wildlife' facts. I'm never sure about some local 'feral creatures' tales and often ask for a re-telling. Toolangi Tiger? Feral pig? Drop bears are definitely aimed at naïve tourists via outback imaginations. Stuck There All Year (S.T.A.Y.), the fibre-glass donation Guide dog who was kidnapped, is not a myth in Antarctica. Just very well photographed in embarrassing situations and helps with morale and fund-raising. Memorable.

Children's authors are especially privileged because often the parents of young readers own the only motel, bed and breakfast or farmstay in that country town. Or the mine is sponsoring the 'cultural' visit, and owns the town.

Few other jobs offer outback travel via chopper or Haulpak mining truck with ginormous wheels and the occasional night in a jail, convent, farm or tent or even a 5-star hotel penthouse on the Gold Coast (the hotelier chain are sponsors of a literary festival).

'You start at 7 a.m. at the school assembly, under the shade. Gets too hot later.'

Everybody knows your schedule in a country town.

'You're staying at X's place.'

Illustrator Michael Salmon frequently tours rural areas. This extract, with his permission, is from an e-mail reply to a local librarian requesting a return visit.

'I remember very well, just how enjoyable was that time spent at X Primary School. Everyone had lots of fun!

I remember also, unfortunately backing into the alabaster statuette of Jesus in the parking bay garden area of the bright blue coloured motel ... run by that (very) upset Italian family!

His head fell off. I offered to re-glue him! But he was never, ever ... quite the same ICON after that!

I noticed on my return Book Week visit that the Motel was for sale ...

I trust that tragic incident didn't bring them bad luck!'
Michael Salmon

Minders

'Minders' are wonderful problem-fixers on tour and the term 'author minder' is bestowed with great respect and affection. They deserve the highest praise for getting an author to the right place on time. Their roles include midnight chauffeuring to radio stations for a talkback audience of insomniacs, shift-workers and prisoners, putting correctly spelled names like 'Jaaiyanne' (pronounced Jane) or Philicitee (Felicity) on yellow stickies for autographing or having the password for the self-locking security door or computer. Not to forget sourcing endless coffee. And when they do all this as if it is a privilege, authors are especially blessed.

De-cluttering my study and filling the recycle bin with paper reminded me of those literary trips I wrote about, immediately after. The others merge in my mind. So this memoir is heavily reliant on published feature articles. And it's a bit weird to re-visit via my own words, as this brings back details, and is a warning that it's vital to write soon after the event, especially if you have a bad memory for dates, distances and times.

Often I remember only the emotion provoked.

Feedback: Poignant & Funny

Re-reading clippings reminded me of meeting an illiterate farmer who learnt to read via my picture book and his Prep-aged kid who acted as literacy tutor.

'Do you have any other books like Hippo? We're reading it together.'

Or reading via a Nepali translator, and having to remember to pause long enough. Or the Blind School in Nanjing when I realised their Braille 'feelie language' was different and my gift of an Australian Braille book was superfluous, but graciously accepted as a novelty.

'Children of the Third Culture' are those students whose parents may be of two different cultures and they are being educated in a third country with its own language. Often these students are fluent in three or four languages. English followed by Spanish and Chinese are the useful international languages now, rather than French.

Keen for their students to hear English spoken with varied accents, some International schools invite authors-in-residence on rotation, from Canada, New Zealand, Britain and Australia.

'English improves our students' chances of getting a good job.'

Literacy in regional Australia is often a worry because lack of skills leads to no confidence and no jobs. So encouraging young blokes and indigenous students to read is a high priority. Thus a male 'sports keen' illustrator is the best role model. A humorous picture-book writer is the next favourite, because illustrations cross cultures more easily than words. Certain adventurous and factual subjects like Antarctica, cycling or trekking will attract non-readers too. I'm not male, nor am I an illustrator, but my collaborators often fit the brief.

There's also the difference between entertainment and an opportunity to talk in depth about motivations, characters and moral dilemmas. If the organiser is expecting instant entertainment and schedules a quiet author after a stand-up comic, that's a recipe for disappointment. But where the audience has had an opportunity to read the author's work beforehand, they ask better questions and elicit thoughtful, genuine answers which make the experience worthwhile for author and audience. Numbers don't always indicate the quality of the questions or answers.

'Only one person turned up. The rest were rent-a-crowd.'

Occasionally in a small group, shy thinkers have a chance to ask about real issues like, 'How do you know to write the way it feels if that happens to you? How come you are writing about the way I feel?'

Passion

'I like to do three 1-hour sessions and then go on life support,' joked passionate social issues novelist Susanne Gervay, who doesn't avoid talking about characters' ways of coping with cancer, grief or bullying.

Loss of voice is an occupational hazard. Bananas, Smoothies or Vitamin C juice are shared remedies to get through heavy speaking schedules of 3–4 venues kilometres apart, plus an evening session for adults. And media interviews on local radio or television.

'Never carry more baggage than can be managed alone, even if you have to decide between fewer knickers or more books. But always pack diplomacy, energy and charm as well as the re-charger,' advised an experienced author. In public authors need to be diplomatic, enthusiastic and appear energetic.

'You can't miss it.' But you can. Or the place has several campuses which have been amalgamated recently and you go to the wrong one which was on the letterhead or e-tag of the invitation.

My tip, when running late, look for the school traffic crossing signs, and the school is probably behind that fence.

By the end of Book Week, most have lost voices and their sense of direction but can't afford to lose their sense of humour.

I enjoy panels and learning from the other participants too. Often the impromptu literary exchanges are genuinely enjoyable for all.

When groups of authors and illustrators tour together around Book, Education or Library Weeks, we learn from each other. That's how I learnt to use 'electronic jewellery' of my e-picture books on a brightly coloured cord around my neck, so I wouldn't leave it behind in the host's computer. Or to invest in a retractable banner of a book cover, for a photo focus instead of a grey wall. Finger puppets. Stickers. Fun stuff kids enjoy.

Wriggle length is about 1 minute for each year of age. Length and content needs to be paced, with fun activities built in, so props help. Even if my pink hippo with his library bag and cake attached has to be safety-belted into the passenger seat of my little car and angled backwards so I can see across his tummy when I do a left-hand turn in traffic. That hippo prop is my weight-lifting exercise. Children compete to be the 'hippo-helper' and carry him, face upright, with respect. That 'prop' was hugged by so many children, he had to be cleaned and sprayed with Scotchgard to prevent further marks, but that's another story.

If unsure, I gamble on calling the librarian 'Jan', as most seem to be called Jan or Lyn or Sue.

Wasted Opportunities

Event mismanagement can lead to exhaustion. Conscientious 'pro' authors tend to 'finish' the badly organised, 'added to' programs.

'Unfair if students miss out,' is their reasoning.

Belatedly I became aware in re-reading my published articles of the subtext of the exhaustion and the disillusionment with lost opportunities if local teachers saw a visiting author as a cheap substitute, didn't prepare the students, or took the day off and lost the chance to discuss with their own students the impact of the visit 'ideas'.

My worst example was being scheduled in a big tent, at a festival next door to a full-on band. Groups of 5–17-year-olds moved through in half-hour sessions, all day until 6 p.m. and not even a cup of tea. A mixed group of adults, teens and toddlers in the same audience is the greatest challenge for a speaker. Especially a group, who can move in and out if they can't see or lose interest.

My shoes sank in the muddy grass; the plastic chair legs stuck, the microphone fused when the storm struck, lights didn't work, powerpoint died, plus the bookseller had no books. Audiences were expecting a magician to entertain. All of us were disappointed.

I've only walked out of one session, which was an extra at the end of a heavy Book Week, in a religious school. I was not introduced, the students were fighting, their teacher had taken the day off and the substitute teacher left and I asked myself, 'What am I doing here?'

So I left. Later the school apologised, but they went on the informal author 'no' list.

Book Week is diet time for me. Hosts provide wonderful meals but often you have to speak between the main course and dessert or even earlier.

Anecdotes are the raw material from which many writers create their books, but often it's the embarrassing events after the book is written which also supply humour.

Author Margaret Clark was e-mailed about a book burglar who had broken into the country school library office. Expensive, hi-tech equipment had been ignored and the Grade 3 culprit took off with valuable items ... three Margaret Clarks and one *Captain Underpants* book. After he was caught and it was explained that he could 'borrow' books from the library, rather than steal them, the young male reader became a readaholic.

Then there was my Sir Galahad. Due to appear as an Ambassador at a distant festival, I checked my map, programmed my GPS and loaded the hippo into the front passenger seat. A big storm and two bad accidents on the freeway meant police stopped traffic for 25 minutes, then re-routed. I had no idea where I was. Jammed in traffic, and my GPS kept sending me back to the freeway entrance and the police blockade. I pulled into a service station and asked for the street names while pulling out the printed map. I rang the festival and no-one was in the office. A customer, Rodney, gallantly spent time orientating me. He put his phone number into my mobile and said he'd guide me in if I was still lost 10 minutes later. He did and I made it only 10 minutes late. Later I called him to thank and offer to send him an e-book of *Trail Magic* which is about the kindnesses strangers offer to travellers. He said there was no need, as he knew who I was and his children had enjoyed my books for years. That's when I remembered the giant hippo on the front passenger seat. So I sent him the e-book anyway. He restored my faith in the kindnesses.

P.J.s

And then there are the strange requests to autograph arms, hands, hats, nappies or even hippo PJs.

> *We found your page after Googling 'Hippo PJs'*
> *We are interested in finding his and hers hippo pajamas and getting them autographed. My wife and I have been looking for such jammies for a long time. Our local Target store has none. Can you point us to where we might find some such as the ones in your Federation Parade photo on your website. Information from the tags on the PJs you found may help? T & M*

Frankly I don't usually wear pajamas, but 30 children in pajamas on a bedtime story book Federation Parade float were to pull the large cake-eating hippo.

Under duress, I was to wear PJs, as two adults were required to anchor the pulling ropes, so the float wouldn't catch in Melbourne tram lines.

Ample nightwear supplies of Teddy Bears, but Hippo pajamas in my size are rare. The helpful Myer store salesgirl found some pink and purple patterned ones. Definitely only nightwear, but I'd be using them in the glare of a Melbourne afternoon, in front of TV cameras in a public parade.

She said the hippo PJs reminded her of her favourite picture book *There's a Hippopotamus on Our Roof Eating Cake*. And had I read that?

'Er ... Yes ... I wrote it.'

Thrilled, she requested that I turn to the TV camera in the parade, and bow so she could see the PJs she sold me. Then she asked me to autograph the credit card and thus pay for the PJs.

Then there was the issue of the missing F.U.D.

A F.U.D. (female urinary device) is standard female clothing issue for Antarctic Division expeditions. Audiences are fascinated by how women manage on the polar ice when there are no toilets and all females want to examine my F.U.D. (which had been washed!) Since my 2001 expedition, I've given lots of conference talks on researching in Antarctica from a female author's perspective, and the F.U.D. is one of my 'props'. But then it was nicked.

> *Dear X,*
>
> *Congratulations on your successful conference.*
>
> *Could you please ask the librarian who 'borrowed' my Antarctic F.U.D. (female urinary device) for a closer look while I was signing copies at the author table of the conference bookstore to please post it to me at the address below, as my need is greater.*
>
> *Perhaps you could put this in your next newsletter? I do use the F.U.D. during my Antarctic talks.*

Reply:

Sent the FUD express post after school today. Ours is a nice beachside suburb like a country town. The postie asked me what I needed to post! I said a female urinary device from Antarctica and showed her. The boss rushed over and said sorry she should have not been so pushy and looked quite worried. All the staff and customers had a look and postie offered to wrap it in bubble wrap. I suggested perhaps not asking so bluntly next time what was being posted.

X

P.S. All now want to buy your 'Antarctic Writer on Ice' book.

Fiction Prediction

Fiction Prediction is when readers insist that something similar to my plot has happened in their real life. I accept this as a compliment, that my plots are well researched or at least feasible. Several have claimed their migrant or refugee grandmother had fake I.D., like the character in my novel *Fake I.D.* Mine was set in the Hungarian revolution of 1956; others claim Fake I.D. in Hong Kong, China and Africa. Others insist snails have eaten their mail, like the picture book *Snail Mail*.

Then there's Fiction Follow-up, when a pet or child is named after a book character. Several ducks are named Stickybeak now. Plus a budgie. And even a Californian wine label.

Such compliments.

'If you have the same name as my character, you're welcome to review my book.'

Several Kyles from *Antarctica's Frozen Chosen* and Zoes from *Muscles* have taken up the offer. No Quentins or Quintanas yet. Yes, I do like Q names.

Experienced authors need to develop a new signature, not the one used on their credit card, as identity fraud can happen. Author bio details used as I.D. are often easily available. One author has the wrong birthdate on all her publicity so her personal ID details cannot be misused. Or that's what she claims.

'Would you like the book to be signed for someone special?'
'For me.'

Occasionally an author may mis-hear or incorrectly write a dedication. Then that book becomes her working copy, unless she meets another reader–client who has a friend with exactly the same name. Any Theobalds out there?

Arriving at the wrong place, being greeted by the wrong name ... being asked to autograph another writer's book:

'Would you sign this please?'
'Sorry, I'm not Andy Griffith.'
'And I didn't write that Bible!'

Or being asked if I knew J.K. Rowling personally? And had I met Harry Potter?

That happens a bit.

Celebs, Fame & Real Heroes

The Australian children's literary community know and respect each other. Fans assume international writers are all close personal friends. 'Don't you know Roald Dahl?'

'No.' It seems crass to explain he's dead.

At least books live beyond the authors' lifespan. That's a comforting thought.

'Varuna' is a writers' retreat in the Blue Mountains bequeathed by the children's author Eleanor Dark. At an international literary festival there, a significant Canadian female author cautioned about the dangers of fame and ego and the different outcomes for males and females on the international circuit. And of the inability to write with compassion once ego takes over.

Often a young male writer who hits the best-seller status early starts to believe his publicist's hype. Has an affair, divorces from family and becomes distanced from the 'real' worlds of which he wrote so well in his first novel. So he can't write a second novel of comparable quality nor earn out his advance. End of promising career, even if his second book is autobiographically about an author on tour.

The irony was that the description fitted one of the current Varuna residents.

'Often a woman has already brought up her family by the time her books are well known or hit best-seller status. She's already established consistent writing habits because she's had to fit around family demands and is in daily contact with non-literary worlds. Problem is not her ego. Older female novelist handles the 'fame' OK, keeps working, but her partner can't cope with the change in status and often they split at his instigation.'

Our young male best-selling international author had gone off to drink with his publicist, so he didn't hear. I wondered how autobiographical was the Canadian author's advice, but didn't like to ask. Googled her later.

CHAPTER 26
ON TOUR

On Tour

May to September is the author travelling and literary festival season.

Residential property may be a good investment due to the mining boom, but intellectual property also enriches a community.

Peripatetic authors have significant and lasting impact on rural communities. Apart from generating business via festival accommodation, catering and transport, they often utilise the settings in later work, and this validates local as worth writing about. Indirectly they help literacy.

If they are versatile and can talk in schools about their work as solo 'ideas' businesses, as well as to special-interest adult groups such as family historians, travel or storytelling groups, they are a worthwhile investment for central funding authorities. The effect of creative people getting together often initiates new cross-media projects, beyond what was planned.

I treasure feedback like this e-mail compiled by a class teacher on her children's ideas on why it would be useful to listen to an author.

- To find out what stuff an author does for work?
- It's good to hear what another person has to say who is not a teacher.
- If we hear authors talk about their books, we might enjoy the books more.
- I'd like to find out how an author gets ideas.

- Maybe I'll find writing a little easier after I listen to an author's ideas.
- To find out how to make lots of money.
- We might want to be an author one day.
- I've never met an author before.
- It's good to find out how other people think.
- To find out what's so good about writing books instead of movies?
- If we like her books, we can ask her to talk about them. That would be good.
- In years to come, we'll be able to say we met someone famous!
- It'll be good because when you read one of her stories, you'll be able to picture her and hear her voice telling the story.
- I didn't like her book much, but she might be ok.

Cathartic Writing

Increasingly, for communities hit by drought or disasters, the value of 'cathartic' writing as a form of therapy is paying off. Writing may not prevent suicide or depression, but it may enable communities to use humour to alleviate distress and provide vicarious experience through the therapy of writing and reading. One writing centre offers cathartic workshops for victims of crime, with a psychologist in the group as well as a writing tutor. Others encourage help with writing the stories of their palliative care patients.

A few schools now have 'Buddies' from the nursing home linking grandparent-aged with young children. Students ask

questions about how life was in earlier times.
'Did you have a wireless?'
'Yes, but a different kind of wi-fi.'

Condobolin festival was started by one female farmer, talking about overcoming rural depression on national radio. Often it takes only one innovator in a rural community to make a significant difference. But then they often move on or burn out.

Western Australia's 'heARTlines' at Mundaring Arts Centre festival had a total of 26 authors and illustrators involved in the schools or public programs and a month-long exhibition of illustrations with a legendary theme, a gallery bookshop and links to workshops at author–activist Katharine Susannah Prichard's former home, with an emphasis on visual–verbal connections. A 'Collaboration' session for the combined authors and artists organisations was included. The availability of books and artwork for sale across a month was significant, enabling follow-up by procrastinators and income for creators. Festivals can stimulate economies beyond their week of programming.

Condobolin's 'Write in the Heart' valued the cathartic effect of local 'yarns' and oral histories in the midst of drought, when autobiographical accounts can help psychologically. Indigenous elders told their stories and adults learnt new 'non-boring' ways of sharing bush yarns for grandchildren in different mediums, whether picture books, audio, blogging, e-mails or mapping. Children attended the library storytelling surrounded by home-made posters of local books.

Electronic innovations mean distance is not a barrier to meeting an author, but the author's keyboard skills may be. During a festival webchat about *Antarctic Writer on Ice* with a Bundaberg school, I deleted them accidentally but we resumed.

What do I remember most from touring?

- The height, health and hi-tech savvy of young Queenslanders whose pastor–principal hoped that in their beachside 'surfing culture' they'd surf with a book in hand!
- Alice, the acknowledged Country Women's Association (C.W.A.) 'best cook' in Condobolin making me 24 profiteroles in exchange for the gift of ideas.
- The deep impact of Barry Heard's candid description of the personal reality of war trauma as a Vietnam veteran, and a silent, totally engrossed and awed adolescent audience.
- Volume fading on live-to-air radio interview and having to 'talk over' to fill dead air space.
- 'Yarning' sessions where even the local pharmacist told his 'coping with the drought' story.
- Messages beeping as I did a left hand turn on the Shire of Bland road (after photographing the REAL Shire of Bland sign named after a local identity) and the mobile resumed after five days outback.
- The long distance 'truckie' telling me he liked to buy 'unabridged' audio stories' which lasted longer.
- Yarning of Aboriginal elders about *Go-Anna!*
- Kiss & Go sign in parent carpark dropping zone.
- Gallery exhibited 'drafts' of *Antarctic Dad* book artwork and a student saying 'I didn't know they had to draw or write it more than once.'

There used to be car number plate labels like State of Excitement. Maybe there should be one for literary festivals? State of Satisfaction or State of Exhaustion?

CHAPTER 27
WRITING HEROES FOR KIDS

What Makes a Hero?

A hero is a person who solves a problem for their community, invents a new way of doing things, makes a significant discovery which benefits the community, or is a role model for the admirable way they live. Or they may be altruistic, and do something at their personal expense of time or health, for the betterment of their community.

'Who is your hero, the one you know personally?'

A 13-year-old former patient nominated his cancer doctor, wrote his answer as a story and gave a copy to his doctor, who was overcome by the response.

Others nominate parents, coaches or teachers.

Despite her being on the $50 banknote, making modest Edith Cowan accessible and attractive to 10-year-olds reading the *Aussie Heroes* series was my challenge. Especially as she rarely photographed well. Historic shots were too formal for today's 'selfie' generation, who are very visual. But I did put her photo on my screensaver for inspiration.

Writing about Weary Dunlop and Fred Hollows was easier because they were active, but I wanted to portray a significant female who had been overlooked.

Writing about modest people who were real heroes is a challenge for an author, especially if the readers are 10-year-olds with little knowledge of the period.

Ask the average 10-year-old, 'Who is your hero?' and they'll probably mention a badly behaved footballer celeb from a recent front page or news feed.

Time to update them with a few facts, but presented

intriguingly. Luckily I had help from researcher Gail.

Much of our history is based on economics. If the person were in a position where their actions had big money consequences, there would be stories written about them. Or if their expertise such as football, music or politics is of interest.

If Edith Cowan had not become the first woman elected to parliament, her other heroic work with child and family welfare would not have even been mentioned. Because she has a university named after her, there's some contemporary relevance. The Fred Hollows eye charity continues internationally, so there's interest in his earlier life too.

Need for Scribes

Are you a hero if others don't know what you've done?
Well-known heroes have usually had a champion or an advocate who was good at writing their facts and getting them out there. Or was terrific at writing genuine eulogies for the funeral, that gave insight into the real contributions during that person's life.

I use 'anecdultery'. That's finding a real mini-story or anecdote about the real person, and use that to support a common thread of ideas which form a theme when writing about the 'quiet hero.'

So one theme might be 'being good with his hands,' like Weary, or 'risk-taking' or 'charming others to your point of view'. With Edith Cowan it was persistence, paperwork and wit. She learnt how to use humour in her speeches. When a politician wanted to double the fare for prams on public transport, she suggested he juggle a baby, toddlers and the groceries for an afternoon in the city, with no other help. He didn't put the pram fare up.

War or sport tends to provide instant conflict. It's much harder to portray cerebral challenge or things going on inside the person's head or during committee meetings (and Edith attended more than her share of those). Too many thoughtful looks on screen, and no action, loses viewers unless you have a voice-over.

Sensationalism can be counter-productive. True, Edith Cowan's father was hanged for the shooting murder of his second wife. But from her teens, Edith did so much to 'make up' and cared for vulnerable children, that's where the emphasis and anecdotes need to be used.

Types of Conflict

Firstly there is the conflict between your character and their environment. This may be a physical environment like the outback, icy Antarctica, or the challenge of building in a difficult terrain.

Or it may be a political or economic environment where your character differs from the major group or wants to change things. Edith Cowan wanted to help families get work and housing but also reduce sexually transmitted disease, which had economic as well as health implications for young children. That was not an appropriate subject at the time for respectable ladies. Even now my publisher edited this to 'infection'.

Secondly, there can be conflict between your character and others. Edith Cowan faced that with the women's political groups who agreed on the types of change needed but not how to best do that.

Thirdly, conflict is required within your character, between what they feel they should do, and what they want to do. We all face this dilemma. A story enables 'weaknesses' to be explored because real life heroes do have weaknesses. I wanted to include Weary's admirable surgical skills but also his bad driving and that he suffered road rage. Youthful readers need to know that even heroes have weaknesses and that admirable traits such as extreme concentration can tip over into obsession. Maybe that is the cost in order for other things to be achieved. Driven personalities may become bossy or develop short fuses.

So the writer has to find humorous anecdotes which indicate

the inner character. Weary demonstrated surgical sewing skills on a sock to medical students. They never forgot that. When Edith finally got elected to parliament in her sixties (as women were not eligible earlier) she gave a nut brooch to each of her supporters, symbolizing a hard nut to crack. And the newspapers of the time satirised her in political cartoons as a housewife with a broom and duster cleaning up the house of parliament.

So dramatised humorous stories, even if occasionally tall stories, are the way to humanise history and share quiet heroes.

Motives matter. So does understanding why someone might have acted that way in those circumstances. That's what provides youth with the opportunity to identify, see things from another perspective and appreciate quiet courage.

In real life, there's lots of boring repetition in any workplace, so any research or problem-solving needs to be constructed as a quest or journey.

Writing a junior history is not less research than writing a full-length book for adults. It's harder. But it may have a wider readership. A book written for children is likely to also be read by adults as an accessible introduction.

History is his and her story. It's about how people solved problems or invented new ways of doing things better. It's also about things going wrong, whether war, prejudice, loss or climactic disasters. History is high gossip about people, not just dead dates and boring facts.

My Challenges in Writing History for 10-Year-Olds

Including a reader-aged child and telling from their perspective, in non-technical vocabulary and to the word limit.

1. An involving perspective. E.g. STAY the Antarctic dog who was dognapped.
2. Distilling extensive research to a few scenes. E.g. In writing *Antarctic Close-Up* about the memorabilia of John Close's

telescope, I read many books about the Mawson expedition and historic Antarctica as well as using my first-hand expedition experience.

3. Non-violent action. Sport or war are overly represented because it's easier to dramatise running or fighting. Much harder to show white lab coats, microscopes and test-tubes as dramatic fact.
4. Oversimplifying good and bad. Life wasn't that simple, but the sentences might need to be.
5. Adding maps and charts.

Using Adventure: Add to- Venture

This means to add venturing to a lifestyle. Take a risk. Try. Physical adventure such as trekking will attract readers initially, but the storytelling still needs a subtext and theme of more substance ... e.g. what are your priorities when conditions are elemental?

Antarctic Action

I went on an Antarctic expedition to find out whether the blokes were running to adventure or away from home. Answer? Both. Unexpectedly I found them to be big readers of other worlds (long winters) and that the creativity to cope with boredom was a required skill, not just physical risk-taking on the ice. Talking about icy physical adventures is a way of attracting readers, plus showing the stunning shots of icebergs, but the real conflict is realisation of human insignificance versus the ability to capture that in words, visuals or science concepts. The symbol of the iceberg with only one tenth showing is relevant.

CHAPTER 28
NOT JUST A PIECE OF CAKE

So You Want to Write for Children?

'It's just a piece of cake' means super-easy in 'old fashioned' phrasing.

'That takes the cake!' means it works.

But writing is not a piece of cake. It's a word diet, for life.

My first choice of memoir title was to indicate the need for fantasy via the absurdity of juxtaposing 'Let Hippos Eat Cake', suggesting permission given to be fanciful, with the querying 'or Not?'. The title is also a clue about dilemmas of being a children's author, long-term. And the misconception that writing for children is a lesser art.

But I changed it to *Not Just a Piece of Cake: Being an Author.*

Here are my 10 diet ingredients for a Memorable Story Recipe

1. Title as first clue
2. Structuring the ideas or choreographing (a bit like a dancing pattern)
3. Characters
4. Underlying conflict to provide the drama
5. Setting: time and place
6. Humour
7. Subtext
8. Twist
9. Credible dialogue

10. Flair, the indefinable quality

If a story has flair you can break all the other rules.
I'll let you into a little secret. It's easy to write a recipe–checklist about what a writer should do. Much harder to apply to a memoir,
A writer needs to stir ideas and emotions.

Realistic Creativity

Being an author is a life sentence, with a few pauses and lots of question marks. Big difference between the euphoria of writing one book and maintaining a workstyle as a writer across decades as well as having a family.
Writing this memoir has been a kind of proof-reading, which I'd previously avoided. Challenges were technical, such as what to include or leave out, and others related to making the content more than ego or a 'how to' write manual. And of themes developing. Until it was written I wasn't aware of the subtext of my father's legacy and how much writers unconsciously build on what went before.
On reflection, I'm grateful for the enriching experiences that being a writer has given me. Relying on precarious creativity is a risk. So was writing this memoir. Because the process about the process needed to be creative too.
Fractals are patterns in nature. I used to dream in fractals regularly but now only sometimes. In this memoir I wanted to explore an author's imaginative life as the story of a quest via a kind of patterning of abstract thoughts, like fractals. Abstractions which others do not see as patterns can be grouped into a design or symbolised into significance.
After my hospitalisation for Streptococcus agalactiae I lost the ability to sustain several levels of story plotting simultaneously, and this memoir was an attempt to re-capture the process ... as participant–observer.

My problem is that I've used several images which have become symbols. There's the idea of cake as inspirational fantasy, but not a constant food, and the idea of a recipe and mixing ingredients.

There there's the idea of a quest or journey and a map of serendipity, where the artist creates the map. Images of hills and plateaux and peaks and rivers and orienteering or structuring a journey. I like 'Questory' as a concept but readers find it obscure.

Then the idea of fractals, of recurring patterns in nature or in dreams, personal ways of mathematically structuring ideas in fiction.

As a writer who thinks in abstract, not pictures, my role is to pull these together to provide a theme or major idea thread in what I have written in the memoir. Since this is also a work in progress for me, I didn't have the theme ready at the beginning, I had to find it during the process of writing the memoir. That was the quest for me, to find a pattern in the random ideas and make sense of my experiences.

My swim-mate Karen said my memoir needed to be 'a story' about the quest of achieving a map of serendipity, the contradiction of creativity and to stress that I dream and think in fractals. Sort of mapping Realistic Creativity with family.

Maybe creating the Map of Serendipity ends here. Now others may use it.

IN PRAISE OF ANECDULTERY

An Author Must Know How Far To Go Too Far.
Hazel Edwards On Why Storytelling Matters.

One of the greatest compliments I ever received was after a web-chat with children from a remote Northern Territory school in the Katherine area. 'Us Mob like your stories: they make us laugh,' they told me.
 Humour is often the way to share an idea or solve a problem. When things go wrong, black humour works—and that is *not* my politically incorrect use of the term. We need to laugh together, not at.
 We all love high gossip: 'why someone did that'. Sometimes it's called history, other times literature or legend. I call it anecdultery. 'Tell us what happened to you when it all went wrong? Why did it happen that way?' Tall tales about human foibles cross cultures.
 I was once Antarctic writer-on-ice in an expedition with 34 blokes and four other women. My first bellydancing class in the beset polar ship in Antarctic (as a creative solution to boredom) was instant icy e-news which grew into folklore Down South. Antarctic expeditioners are the *best* tall story tellers, problem-solvers, big book readers (long winters) and risk-takers since they have an overdose of the adventure gene.
 Storytellers have to be risk-takers too. An artist must know how far to go too far. Storytelling can be a risky business, especially if you show unpopular truths or minority viewpoints via satire, fantasy or mythology. A deceptively simple story may illustrate a complex idea or a productive life.
 Although I'm not a genealogist, I can pronounce and spell the word. I've been involved in *Writing a Non-Boring Family*

History workshops for 'genies' for years. It's about ways of crafting the extraordinary ordinary stories of family who were too busy living to keep extensive diaries; histories and herstories that are worth telling. A regional newspaper, which must remain nameless, wrote me up as gynaecologist Hazel Edwards. When I pointed out the error, and that I was not a genealogist nor a gynaecologist, she said "Oh it's the story of one end of life or the other".

Crafting anecdotes into a story helps families who want to know why their ancestors travelled that far or that way. Stories can be therapy for the creator or for the audience, but they must be crafted to work well. If the tone is genuine, compassion is evident and the story needs to be told, it will last. But autobiographical exercises in chronological boredom should be avoided.

A story may travel further than its creator. Like grown-up children, book stories have to go out on their own. Sometimes they adapt well into other languages, media or times. Occasionally they don't.

A creator must judge success by internal criteria: the gap between the aspiration and the creation. What was the goal? Was it reached? How can it be done differently and more effectively the next time?

Did they laugh? Did they ask questions? Did they leave and do something differently the next day? If so, was your story thought-provoking, entertaining or propaganda?

It has been said: *an artist must know how far to go too far*. Creators are our dream-makers, those who suggest new perspectives, which may influence government, politics, management, health or the arts.

To influence reality, dreams must be structured and shared in a format others can understand. My grandmother taught me to read before I went to school. My father told me stories. I write a story for my grandson each birthday, but the format may change. Now it is electronic. I have several co-writers and many colleagues whose skills support me.

Today storytelling may be on Ipod, on web chat via interpreters or by yet-to-be invented smellovision but we all need to know is what happened to others and why, preferably with a bit of a humorous twist.

Read one story per month from another culture. That's my new aim. Recently I was in Nanjing, China, as cultural exchange author and given a beautiful book by a young adult novelist but I could read only her photo on the cover. That's why translations also matter.

The ASA medal brooch is a brand of storyteller across cultures, and I accept it, on behalf of all apprentice bards with awareness of the honour paid by the ASA and the creators of this work of art.

This is an edited version of an acceptance speech given for the 2009 ASA Medal, which is awarded biennially in recognition of an outstanding contribution to the Australian writing community.

COPYRIGHT

Copyright © Hazel Edwards 2015

First published in 2015 by Brolga Publishing

This edition published in 2023
by Ligature Pty Limited

PO Box 294 · Balmain NSW 2041 · Australia
www.ligatu.re · mail@ligatu.re

e-book ISBN 978-1-922749-56-7
print ISBN 978-1-922749-25-3

All rights reserved. Except as provided by fair dealing or any other exception to copyright, no part of this book may be reproduced or transmitted in any form or by any means without permission in writing from the publisher.

The moral rights of the author are asserted throughout the world without waiver.

ligature *un*tapped

www.ingramcontent.com/pod-product-compliance
Lightning Source LLC
Chambersburg PA
CBHW030111100526
44591CB00009B/360